Rebuilding Your Temple Garden

By Stacy Mal

Certified Health Coach

Blogger/Author

Plexus Worldwide Ambassador

Independently Published

North East, PA USA

www.RebuildingYourTemple.com

Adapted from the book *Victory in the Spiritual Garden*

Originally Published by Stacy Mal, December 2016

Pennsylvania, USA

Independently Published

North East, PA 16428

www.RebuildingYourTemple.com

www.MilitiaOfMary.com

ISBN # 9798708603265

To the Blessed Virgin Mary,

from the bottom of my heart.

TABLE OF CONTENTS

CHAPTER ONE: AN INTRO TO THE JOURNEY.................5

CHAPTER TWO: THE MAP.....................................10

CHAPTER THREE: THE GATE 26

CHAPTER FOUR: THE DOOR OF MARY 41

CHAPTER FIVE: THE WEEDS.................................54

CHAPTER SIX: THE THORNS.................................66

CHAPTER SEVEN: THE DIRECTION & BLOOMS 79

CHAPTER EIGHT: THE EMBRACE & THE TREE...........96

CHAPTER NINE: THE CALL 112

Chapter One: An Intro to the Journey

This book reminds me of an incident that happened years ago. I was driving my two oldest daughters to a craft store. We were living in a town that we had JUST moved to, so I was not familiar with where I was going. So I relied on Siri, my cell phone navigator, to get me there.

We drove for approximately forty-five minutes or so. I had little cell signal and was growing concerned. All of a sudden, Siri announced, "You have arrived." The problem was, we were in the middle of a highway, in the middle of nowhere, with no craft store in sight. There was not even an exit to get off at. Clearly, we had **_not_** arrived. Clearly, Siri was wrong. We had unknowingly gone the wrong way for a long time. And we had been duped by the robot woman in my phone.

Now what? It was Sunday, and the store (wherever it was) would be closing soon. I had no other map. I had little cell signal, and now, very little battery left.

That craft store journey reminds me of this book because it shows the importance of having a reliable map and a trustworthy guide. This is especially true in the spiritual journey, where so much takes place in an unseen dimension. Without assistance, how could we ever make it to our Heavenly destination? We simply couldn't.

Thankfully, God has not left us wandering. Since the beginning of time, he has directed us through Jesus, Mary, the prophets, and the Holy Spirit. Each of their words is like a brushstroke. And in this book, they come together to form a detailed, topographic map to lead you through this world. And no, the guide is not me. It is the Holy Spirit -- the breath of the all-knowing God -- who inspired me to "draw" it for you in these pages.

There is still one more reason why that story reminds me of this book. On the way to the craft store that day, I put all my trust in my phone... in a small piece of man-made equipment. I was confident it would get me there because, after all, it was the newest "advanced technology." But it failed me.

I wonder how many others have sought out "the way" through man-made things. I wonder how many others are confidently being led down the highway of life by _worldly_ ideas. I wonder how many others will have to come to the harsh reality that they've been traveling the wrong way and that they've been duped by the father of lies. I wonder how many others will be shocked to find that time is quickly running out, that it's almost closing time for this earthly life.

I personally have had this experience, friends -- and no, I'm not talking about my experience on the way to the craft store. I had an "awakening" of sorts back in 2006. I took a trip to Maranatha Spring and Shrine, the home of Holy Love Ministries, located in Elyria, Ohio. (Ironically, I got lost on the way there, too. I'm not kidding. I did. But that's a story for another day.)

During that pilgrimage, I opened my heart to the messages that Jesus and Mary were giving to a visionary named Maureen Sweeney Kyle. Through these messages, I came to understand that I had been journeying way off course. I had been walking the "wide way that leads to perdition" (Matthew 7:13). I was following blind guides (Matthew 15:14), and I needed to get back on track.

Not long after my first visit to Maranatha Spring and Shrine, I participated in a seven-week Catholic Charismatic seminar called "Life in the Spirit," where I renewed my baptismal vows and prayed for a deeper indwelling of the Holy Spirit. After that, I began to keep a prayer journal, and the Lord began to speak to my heart in those pages. He began confirming the truth of the Holy Love messages and the dire importance of them during these times.

I came to see that this "map" was not just for me. It was to be shared and distributed to other wandering souls. So *that* is the reason for this book. But, please, understand: just because I possess the map and have *begun* the journey, that is not to say, "I have arrived" (like Siri said). Clearly, I have not. I am still traveling. I am still far off. But I know the way, now.

"I am the Way, the Truth and the Life," Jesus said in John 14:6.

Friends, I have tried so many other ways that led to nowhere (like my craft store trip). Now, I finally know the _right_ way, and I am looking for some fellow travel companions if you are up for the journey? It is a journey like no other; I can promise you that. It's absolutely life-changing. Or, should I say afterlife-changing.

But don't take this lightly. The message/map presented in this book is something that is weighing heavily and mightily on

God's heart. I know because, when He laid it on my heart, it was powerful. As I began putting it to paper, it was like a raging river, once held back by a small dam that was finally being released. Whoosh!!! It came with power to the page. And my goodness, I came up against a lot of resistance writing this, which only confirmed how important this message really is.

I say this, so you know that you are reading this for a very specific reason. God has called you to this moment individually, to meet you personally, to embrace you softly, and speak to you powerfully. Believe that. This is not some haphazard occurrence. So, I'm asking you to open your heart as you read so that you can receive this important message and let it take root in you.

"Today if you hear his voice, harden not your hearts." (Heb 3:15)

Meditation

"Child, salvation is the gift of the Resurrection bought and paid for by My Son, offered to you in every moment for all time. Ponder where you were, My child, and where you are now. Imagine the heights to which I still can take you. You did nothing to deserve this gift, and I am not obligated to give it. But My Love provokes it. My Heart yearns for you to have it...Child, ponder this road. Ponder how lost you were. Ponder how hopeless you were. Hope, child, hope. This is the soft breeze that blows along the path, refreshing you. It is what makes this road feel different from every other road. My children need hope. Tell them what you have found on this road. Tell them where it has led you. Tell them Who it is that accompanies you on the journey. Tell them of Me, child. Tell them of [the] gift.

Give them hope." *(An excerpt from "Mornings with my Father" by Stacy Mal.)*

Prayer:

Lord God, I open my heart to the journey you are calling me to. Be with me on this passage, and grant me wisdom to understand the way. Grant me perseverance and strength to continue until my arrival at the blessed destination. It is my desire and my will to travel this way. Assist me at every step. This I pray in Jesus' Name. Amen.

Scripture

"They said to him, 'Consult God, that we may know whether the journey we are making will lead to success.' The priest said to them, 'Go in peace! The journey you are making is under the eye of the LORD.'" (Judges 18:6)

Questions for Reflection

Am I determined and resolute in beginning this spiritual journey?

Are there any doubts or reservations currently in my heart that would make this journey difficult?

What steps can I take today to overcome these reservations?

Is there a trusted friend who I can ask to pray for me as I begin this journey?

Chapter Two: The Map

"The soul may spend a lifetime searching for a way into the Divine Will of My Father. All the while, I offer him the straight and narrow path of the journey through the Chambers of Our United Hearts. To know of this journey is a great grace. To know of it but refuse to travel it further wounds My Most Mournful Heart. A soul can be saved without making the spiritual journey through these Sacred Chambers, but it is more difficult. That would be like searching for a treasure after you throw away the map. The treasure, in this case, is union in My Father's Divine Will."

~Jesus to Maureen, June 5, 2016

So, why did I choose the title "Victory" for this book? Well, for a couple of reasons. One, you read in the last chapter that this book is to serve as a roadmap to Heaven. Victory simply means you have arrived at your destination. But there are other reasons also.

Victory is a word that reminds me of a very dear friend of mine. Her name was Patti. It was a word she heard in prayer during her journey with breast cancer, up until her death in August 2013. I was privileged enough to witness the way she lived out much of what I'm going to write about. This book is the map, but Patti was a traveler. She took the map and ran with it. Right up to the pearly gates. She tested it out and confirmed its truth. I believe she "arrived," as Siri would say. And so, I will write more about Patti in later chapters to explain this.

The third reason why I chose "Victory" as the title is to give you hope. Many people nowadays are getting discouraged -- with life, relationships, tragedies, the world. Every time we turn around, it seems there is another friend or family member abandoning the faith for opposing ideas, or there is another restriction placed on Christians.

It's clear that there is a movement in the world right now to silence (even to overthrow and dismantle) Christianity -- one law, one belief, one heart at a time. It's a movement led by the devil to rid creation of the Creator. But, I am here to tell you: that will _not_ happen.

I am here to tell you; you needn't be discouraged. In this book, I will reveal to you a secret, protected, safe haven that leads to victory. It's the one place where governments cannot rule over, the one place where atheistic policies have no control, the one place where the devil himself cannot touch. That place, my friends, is in the depths of the human heart.

Deep within each of us, there is a place -- a secret place -- untouchable by the world, by government, by circumstance, time, or space. It is a dwelling place, created _by_ God, _for_ God, and it looks something like the cover of this book. This is the map. This is where the journey of life _really_ takes place -- in a secret, spiritual garden inside the human person.

Now, I know the image is rudimentary. This is my feeble (VERY feeble) attempt at trying to create a visual for what I want to explain in these pages. It was quite difficult trying to capture a mystical paradise that's technically _beyond_ our imagination. So, bear with me.

This garden inside each of us is designed to flow with the Living Water and shine with the Light of the Son of God. It is an _eternal_ garden. Everything on earth is passing. Everything. Trees die; flowers die; bodies die... but what God plants in the human heart (what He prunes and waters and grows in the human heart) bears fruit for all eternity.

The question is: do you know it's inside of you? Is the secret garden in you cleared by frequent foot traffic? Is it cared for and cultivated by God, blooming with grace, full of life, and bearing fruit? Or is it neglected, deserted, and overgrown?

Is the secret garden in you an abandoned temple or a thriving kingdom? For most of us, it is an abandoned temple to some degree. We are somewhere in between, primarily because we are fallen creatures from Adam and Eve. We live in a difficult and very busy world, and the devil is strong at work around us. But that's ok. In this book, we are going to focus on rebuilding the temple. We are going to survey the property and set out to bring back the garden.

Romans 12:1 says, _"let God transform you inwardly."_ And that's exactly what we're going to do. Because, when your garden becomes a thriving Kingdom -- with the great, almighty King of Kings sitting on the throne of your heart -- you WILL overcome any enemy that sets out against you. You will. But, if this garden is an overgrown, abandoned temple that you hardly ever set foot in, you will likely be brought down by any enemy that sets out against you.

Friends, your Heavenly Victory depends solely on the state of this garden and your place in it.

So, over the next several chapters, I want to discuss this garden with you. But I don't want to just _discuss_ it. I want us to actually _go_ there. We are going to use the map on the front cover, and we are going to journey deep into its many levels. We will journey from the dark outer area through the gate into weeds and thorns, then into buds and blooms, straight to the Tree of Life -- to Jesus Himself, who is united with the Father, in the Holy Spirit. We are going to seek and encounter the living God, the Most Holy Trinity, right here in the very depths of ourselves. Consider this your DIY at-home retreat.

Perhaps, though, you're thinking, _"A garden? Levels? Whaaat am I getting into with this book?"_ Well, let me put you at ease by saying this is _not_ a new concept. Well, the idea of a garden is new, yes. Or at least I think it is. It's new to me. God laid the garden on my heart a few years ago in my prayer journal and has been teaching me about it ever since, almost every time I go to prayer.

But the spiritual journey inside the human person is _not_ a new concept. It's in scripture (Old and New Testaments). Many saints have also spoken about it (St Francis de Sales and St. Teresa of Avila -- both doctors of the Church -- are the ones that I will reference). And the Blessed Mother herself is even speaking about it in modern-day apparitions. (I will primarily mention the messages given to Maureen Sweeney Kyle at Holy Love Ministries in Elyria, Ohio.)

Scripture, the saints, and the Blessed Mother all talk about this journey and its many levels -- each in a unique way -- but it's all the same message. It's all the same journey, the same map, the same levels. St. Francis de Sales calls the levels "parts" in his book _The Introduction to the Devout Life_. St. Teresa of Avila calls them "rooms" in her book *Interior Castle*. And the Blessed Mother calls them "chambers" in Her messages given to Maureen.

They're all talking about this one journey but in different ways. So, if you're still skeptical about the garden, understand that it's supported by Scripture, doctors of the Church, and the Blessed Mother Herself. So, you can take it up with them. ;)

Now, back to the garden. Contrary to what it looks like in the image on the cover, the spiritual garden is _not_ small or confined. It takes our entire life to journey through it. And even though it's inside of us, it's not physical or material either. The garden is actually a _portal_ into another dimension, the spiritual dimension. This portal is full of little passageways that take you deeper and deeper into the fullness of God, into the depths of the Holy Trinity.

Now, you're probably thinking, *"What? Into the depths of God? I thought you said the garden was in the depths of the human person?"*

YES, I did. The truth is, it's both. Listen, here's the thing: at Baptism, the Catechism of the Catholic Church says you were "incorporated into Christ." (#1272) You became a temple of the Holy Spirit (#1265). You became a partaker in the "divine life" of God the Father (#1265). Think about that for a moment -- and I mean _really_ think about that. You share in the divine life of God the Father. You're integrated into the Son. The Holy Spirit dwells within you... not in your _physical_ heart, but in the garden, _spiritually_.

Friends, when God gave you physical life at conception, He put you inside a universe. But when He gave you spiritual life at

Baptism, He put a universe inside of you. Imagine it: at Baptism, an "imperishable seed" (as the Catechism calls it, #1228) comes down from Heaven and takes root in the human person... and an eternal garden springs forth.

In John 3:5, Jesus said, *"In all truth, I tell you, no one can enter the kingdom of God without being born through water and the Spirit."* He's talking about Baptism.

So understand: this journey is both a journey into the depths of yourself and into the depths of God... because, if God is _in_ you, then in order to get to God, you must go inward. Make sense? To go deeper and deeper into God means to go deeper and deeper into yourself.

Now, I am _not_ saying you need to focus solely on yourself. When I say "go inward" into yourself, I'm not talking about putting yourself first. I'm not condoning selfishness or the "*me, me, me*" mentality -- those are actually things that hinder the spiritual life.

No. What I'm talking about is withdrawing from everything outside in the world and going inside into silence. I'm talking about prayer, recollection, meditation. I'm talking about focusing on God (not on self) but doing it inside.

Friends: if we hope to experience the Victory, this must -- and I mean must -- be learned and practiced, _often_. I cannot stress this enough. This is the very crux of the spiritual journey: silence, prayer, meditation.

This is what Jesus is talking about in the story of the true disciple found in Matthew 7 (which starts at verse 21). *Jesus said, "Not everyone who says to me, 'Lord, Lord,' will enter the*

Kingdom of Heaven, but only the one who does the will of my Father in Heaven. Many will say to me on that day, 'Lord, Lord, did we not prophesy in your name? Did we not drive out demons in your name? Did we not do mighty deeds in your name?' Then I will declare to them solemnly, 'I never knew you. Depart from me, you evildoers.'"

"I never knew you." Wow. Those are strong words for someone who's been driving out demons and doing mighty deeds. *"Not everyone who says to me 'Lord, Lord' will enter the Kingdom of Heaven."* Think about that! Please, think about that. These people call Him "Lord." They essentially work for the Church. But they can't enter the Kingdom of Heaven?

This is because our spiritual journey is _not_ just about what we say and what we do. It's about the garden. Those disciples lived outside the garden in the dark area. They lived in the world. They kept busy doing many good deeds in His name, mostly for show, but they never went inward to where He was actually at. They never spent time with Him in prayer and recollection. They knew _about_ Him, but they never really knew _Him_.

Now, Jesus was not saying that good works and mighty deeds and prophesying are not good or important. No. What He's saying is that these things should be an extension -- a _fruit_ -- of your relationship with Him. They should be a _result_ of the bond you have with Him, which can only be formed inwardly, in the garden.

Now...yes, God is so good that He will allow people that don't know Him to perform mighty deeds in His name. But, it's for the sake of bringing others to Him. There are priests, living in mortal sin, who still bring Jesus to us in the Eucharist. But, when it comes down to _your_ spiritual life when it comes to _your_ salvation, it's absolutely dependent upon _your_ bond and connection with Jesus.

True Christianity is not an organization, an association, a social status, or a club. It's a relationship! So please understand how important this is. This garden, this spiritual universe, this portal -- _this_ is your eternity. Your body will die -- it will. But _this_ is eternal. This will last forever.

Do you hear what I'm saying? This eternal garden, friends, is the Kingdom of Heaven. The Tree of Life in the center of the Garden is the victory -- the goal of all goals, the heights of Heaven, the depths of God! It's the big, red X on the map—the destination. And yes, that's right, Heaven begins inside of you, RIGHT NOW, while you're on earth. It's the foretaste... yes, the victory.

This is important to understand. We don't know when our last day will be or how long we have on earth, but I can tell you, wherever you're at (inside or outside the garden) on the day that you die... well, _that_ determines where you spend eternity.

1 John 5:12 confirms this, _"Whoever possesses the Son has life; whoever does not possess the Son of God does not have life."_

2 Thessalonians 1:9 says, _"These will pay the penalty of eternal ruin, separated from the presence of the Lord and from the glory of his power."_ This, quite simply, is Hell.

Some people have a hard time with this idea that God -- a good, merciful God -- sends people to Hell. But He doesn't _send_ us. Friends, we _choose_ it. He judges, yes, but when the curtain is lifted, and the veil of life is removed, and you're standing outside the gate, His justice simply pronounces what is. He simply proclaims, _"You are here."_ Or, as Scripture says, _"I never_ *knew you."* We then remain there, where we chose in life -- for all of eternity.

Now, let's look at the garden. This, friends is the New Jerusalem. This garden is "the future city" spoken about in the Bible. In the Old Testament (beginning at Ezekiel 40), the New Jerusalem is Ezekiel's prophetic vision of a city that is to come. It is a city that is centered around the _rebuilt_ Holy Temple. According to Ezekiel, it will be inhabited by people living eternally in _spirit_ form.

In the New Testament, Saint John also describes the New Jerusalem in the book of Revelations (Chapter 21). Both Ezekiel and John are taken _in spirit_ to God's Holy Mountain, where they see the city. (John sees it descending from Heaven.) This has long been seen as a symbol of the Church descending to earth, and rightly so. Through the Church -- through Baptism -- the garden city comes down from Heaven and takes root in the human heart.

The garden city is for God, by God, with God. It's a dwelling place for Him and us. In 2 Corinthians 6:16, Paul says: *"For we are the temple of the living God; as God said: 'I will live with them and move among them, and I will be their God, and they shall be my people.'"*

I relay this not to confuse you or get too theological, but simply to help you understand how important this is. You don't necessarily need to understand the details of the New Jerusalem, but please understand that this garden we are about to journey through was revealed by God thousands of years ago to a prophet named Ezekiel. It was also shown to the apostle John. It was shown to Saints and visionaries throughout the ages. It's even been revealed to a sinner like me. God is repeating this message because it's so very, _very_ important.

Revelations describes why it is important. _"I also saw the holy city, a new Jerusalem, coming down out of Heaven from God, prepared as a bride adorned for her husband. I heard a loud voice from the throne saying, 'Behold, God's dwelling is with the human race. He will dwell with them, and they will be his people, and God himself will always be with them [as their God]. He will wipe every tear from their eyes, and there shall be no more death or mourning, wailing or pain, [for] the old order has passed away.'"_

Let's look at that "old order" for a minute. Let's look at the old garden, that first garden, which is the Garden of Eden found in the book of Genesis. We know that Adam and Eve are "types," meaning they foreshadow or prefigure the "new Adam and the new Eve," who are Jesus and Mary. But the same is also true for the _dwelling place_ of Adam and Eve.

The Garden of Eden (in the first book of the Old Testament) prefigures the new garden, the new Jerusalem (in the last book of the New Testament). And like most "types" or figures, the real one far surpasses the thing that prefigured it. In other words, this new garden will surpass Eden as much as Mary surpasses Eve or as much as Christ surpasses Adam. In other words, this garden is the real deal, folks. Like I said before, it's so very important.

Revelations 21 continues, _"The one who sat on the throne said, 'Behold, I make all things new.' Then he said, 'Write these words down, for they are trustworthy and true.' He said to me, 'They are accomplished. I [am] the Alpha and the Omega, the beginning and the end. To the thirsty, I will give a gift from the_ *spring of life-giving water. The VICTOR will inherit these gifts, and I shall be his God, and he will be my son. But as for cowards, the unfaithful, the depraved, murderers, the unchaste, sorcerers, idol-worshipers, and deceivers of every sort, their lot is in the burning pool of fire and sulfur, which is the second death.'"*

He makes all things new, friends. Listen, there was no "Plan B." God's original plan was to live with His children for all eternity in the garden of paradise, in His kingdom... and He _will_, even after the fall of Adam and Eve. Do you see now what Jesus accomplished? Nailed to the Tree of Life, He re-opened the garden for souls!! He brought the garden of life into the untouchable dimension of the human heart.

 In the old garden, Adam and Eve sinned, and they were banned from the garden. God put angels outside Eden to keep them out, to keep them away from the Tree of Life. Today there are angels -- your guardian angels and the archangels, St. Michael especially -- drawing us *into* the new garden, TOWARDS the _new_ tree of life, which is the Real Presence of Jesus.

This is what His sacrifice bought for us! He bought us another chance!! So how do we get there? Matthew 7:7 says simply, *"Ask and it will be given to you...seek, and you will find...knock and the door will be opened unto you."* Sounds simple, right? Well, it _is_ actually that simple. God is not unreachable. He is not unattainable. He is here, inside each of us, now, always.

Friends, if you want to be in God's presence. Then, _be_ in God's presence. Psalm 46 says. *"Be still and know that I am God."* That's it. It's that simple. Meditate on this scripture. Recite it often. Let it become, inside of you, the _living_ Word that it is.

Be still and know that I am God.

Be still and know I am.

Be still and know.

Be still.

Be.

Just *be* with Him. You don't need to speak a lot of fancy words. Just go to the garden. Picture it in your mind and just sit there. Find a quiet place and withdraw from the world for a minute. Turn off your cell phone, the TV, the computer. And sit in silence. <u>*Silence*</u>. Do we even know what that is anymore?

Listen, friends. The Devil attacks silence so ruthlessly these days because he knows if you never have silence or recollection -- if you never enter inward into prayer -- then you will never enter God. If you never enter God, then the devil has you in the palm of his hand!!

Nowadays, it's like "the devil's pentecost" out there in the world. Instead of a mighty wind bringing peace and life and power, the devil brings a mighty wind of busy-ness and chaos and unrest and anxiety. Instead of tongues of fire that enflame hearts, the devil brings a fire that leaves us completely burned out.

We have become so accustomed to noise, to the constancy of stimuli, that soon, this will become a habit for us, and noise will become a "need." Soon, silence and stillness will become so foreign to us that it will be torture for us to sit in it. Then how will we ever find God?

This is the devil's plan!! Do not be tricked. Do not be distracted. Make silence a priority. Set your phone alarm as a reminder for noon, 3 PM, and 6 PM with just the word "garden." Then turn off your cell phone and sit. When you're driving, turn off the radio. Learn to look for little moments of quiet. Learn to love silence.

Listen to the still small voice of God, calling you. Leaders of nations may try to rid the world of God, of His Church, and His laws... but no mortal on earth can take away the secret garden. No law can shut down, close up, or condemn the garden of your heart. Let the Kingdom of God come into the world through the hearts of His children!! God, Himself has deemed it so. He has designed it this way. He shall restore His people. He shall make new His Church. And it will be resurrected in the deep... in the garden.

And please know: I am not writing this book from a "teaching" perspective. I'm not writing from my mind. I am writing from my heart. I am writing from personal experience. As I said before, God began to teach me about the garden years ago. And at the time, I was struggling desperately with a very close, unhealthy relationship. And to be honest, it was destroying me.

I was tied to this person's rollercoaster, getting flipped upside down, sinking to new lows -- daily. I remember running to the mall on a Holy Saturday. At the time, our diocese had a chapel set up in the local mall, and there were confessions being held there that day. I ran into that chapel, and I spewed all kinds of ugliness from my broken heart on the poor priest.

He sat there very calmly and just stared at me. When I was done, he said very softly, "God is about to roll away the stone in your life." That was it.

I thought, *"WHAT? That's it? That's all he's got for me? Didn't he hear what I said?!"*

Well, the next morning (Easter Sunday), I got up early (before anyone else in the house was awake), and I sat on my couch. I had no words, no prayer. I was *that* distraught. So I just put myself in the garden. I went into the deep, into silence. And, I don't know how to tell you this, but the Almighty God met me there. I could feel His power embrace me, hug me... and not just me as a whole. It was like He hugged every cell in my body. He filled me and stretched me with new life. It was exactly like the priest said. God rolled away the stone that Easter morning -- and He resurrected me, right there with bed head, in my PJs. He resurrected me in the garden.

I didn't have the perfect prayer, the perfect disposition. I didn't even have a right heart at the time, truth be told. But in the quiet, I went to some secret, unknown place with only the hope of meeting Him. And He came -- with *power* from on high.

So please, please understand when I say you have been called here too. It's not just that you have been called to read this book. Friends, you've been called to the garden. You have been called to victory.

Do not be disheartened, friends. God is here and will be, always. No matter what you're going through right now... no matter what the WORLD goes through. If the world removes His law from buildings, He will write it on their hearts. If they remove His name from policies, He will write it on their foreheads. If they ban Him from classrooms and courtrooms, He will come with greater power into homes and families. But it all starts in the garden. In silence, and in hearts. Understand that. Believe that.

This moment, right here, right now, begins a new life for you. And the devil is threatened. He will come against you with every reason why you should not continue reading this book and making this retreat. He will stir up chaos and distractions. He will tempt you with other things that suck the hours and minutes from your day until nothing is left for reading. But persevere, my friends. Resist the devil and make this journey a priority at all costs. Are you with me?

Meditation

"Child...I desire you become so familiar with the garden that this becomes your home. Come here as often as you can. How it pleases me that you come to me. How I dread sitting in the garden alone... It was made for our communion. Come here when you receive me in the Eucharist, child. Come here in your thoughts during the day, and I will meet you. I will speak to you. I wait for you. We have so much to accomplish together. We need the time to converse. You need the time to be filled with grace and strength. Much, much depends on this. The garden of your heart, child, is so beautiful. I created it with My own Hand. Let us care for it together. Let us enjoy it together -- you and me -- each day, for all eternity. Each day I plant anew. Come, see what I am doing... in you, with you, for you. I am giving back the garden before the fall. See, child, it is within you. I am here, within you. Come and live. Alleluia, alleluia!" *(An excerpt from "Mornings with my Father" by Stacy Mal.)*

Prayer

Lord, God, I come to you in the stillness and quiet, in the garden of my heart, with the hopes of entering your presence. Receive me, Oh Lord. Embrace me. I am Yours, and You are mine. Open my heart that I may make this journey and reach the destination you have ordained for me. Jesus, I trust in you. Jesus, I love you. Amen.

Scripture

" The LORD is my shepherd; there is nothing I lack. In green pastures, he makes me lie down; to still waters, he leads me; he restores my soul. He guides me along right paths for the sake of his name. Even though I walk through the valley of the shadow of death, I will fear no evil, for you are with me; your rod and your staff comfort me. You set a table before me in front of my enemies; You anoint my head with oil; my cup overflows. Indeed, goodness and mercy will pursue me all the days of my life; I will dwell in the house of the LORD for endless days." (Psalm 23)

Questions for Reflection

When you look inside yourself, do you see a thriving Kingdom or an abandoned temple?

What is the most difficult thing about trying to find quiet time with God? What are the primary distractions and obstacles?

What part of the day would be easiest for me to enter the garden? Morning, noon, or night?

What steps can I take today to ensure I have time each day to enter the garden?

Chapter Three: The Gate

"Once again, I have come to remind you of Satan's tactics in the world. He obscures the line between good and evil, making choices for or against sin ambiguous. This is why I have been telling you that sin must be clearly defined as sin from the pulpit. It is up to Church leaders to define evil - not to accommodate evil."

~ Blessed Mother to Maureen, April 14, 2016

Now that we have talked about where the garden is and why it's important, I'd like to actually go inside it. And I'm going to just preface this... from here on out, I'm going to be real with you. We're not tip-toeing around the garden. Okay? If you want to rebuild your temple, if you want to bring back the garden and make it to the center, that's great. I'm going to give you the map, and I'm going to support you, but I'm NOT going to downplay it or sugar coat it.

This, friends is the narrow way. It's going to be work. It's going to be truth. It's going to be hard. But I hope you'll stick with me because it's worth every single step.

Okay, I mentioned it before, and I'll say it again -- inside this garden is symbolic of being in a "state of grace." Now, what is a state of grace? Some of you have probably heard this term before. Basically, it's living free of mortal sin. Mortal sin (serious sin) puts you outside the garden in the dark area (*"where there is grinding and gnashing of teeth,"* as it says in Matthew 13:42). It's death to your soul. A state of grace, on the other hand, is *life* to your soul.

Simply put: a "state of grace" is inside the gate, deserving Heaven. A state of mortal sin is outside the gate, deserving Hell. Make sense? To truly take this journey, then, we must live free of serious sin.

OK. Now, am I saying that you can't enter prayer or enter "inward" if you're not in a state of grace? No, absolutely not.

Anyone can pray in any state. In fact, a person in mortal sin, praying for mercy, is probably one of God's most beloved prayers. It's the sound of a child returning to Him. It's what He longs for. However, the garden experience _is_ different in mortal sin. When you're outside a state of grace (living in mortal sin), it's like standing on the edge of the gate, looking in. You experience the garden like _"oh, look at the beauty of the living water"_ versus actually getting your feet wet, drinking it, taking it into your body, and allowing it to have a real effect on you.

It's like saying, _"look at how beautiful the flowers are"_ versus smelling their sweetness, touching the soft, velvety petals, and being healed by their aromatherapy. You _can_ pray in a state of mortal sin. You _can_ experience the garden to some degree outside a state of grace, but it's not fully how God intended it for you. It's more from the standpoint of a spectator than a participant.

The disciples who we mentioned earlier (who did mighty deeds but did not _know_ Jesus), these disciples knew _of_ the garden from this standpoint.

So you see, I couldn't have just stopped after the last chapter. Just talking _about_ the garden, just _looking_ at the garden is simply not enough. Knowing about it doesn't get you anywhere in the spiritual journey. YOU HAVE TO ACTUALLY ENTER IT.

But, in order to enter it, you have to be in a state of grace. In order to be in a state of grace, you have to avoid mortal sin. Plain and simple. I wish I could tell you there was another way, an easier way. But there isn't. You must be free of mortal sin.

 Ahhh.... sin. How little we speak of this word anymore. How fearful we are sometimes to even utter it in certain circles, lest we be considered intolerant or judgmental. What's worse: many people today do not even believe such a thing exists anymore. Or, if they _do_ believe sin exists, they think it exists only as an _extreme_, something no one really ever commits except serial killers and other monsters.

Let me just say: WOE TO YOU, if you are one of the people who think this way!! WOE TO YOU, because the devil has you _exactly_ where he wants you.

Friend, if you are one of these people, the devil has you thinking there's no gate, there's no separation between life and death, and therefore no need for pursuing life, no need for entrance within. He's basically rendered you immobile in the journey, chained to darkness by the error of your mind. Listen, I'm not condemning you or judging you. I am speaking to you as one who cares for your soul... as one who knows the danger, from personal experience.

I was one of these people who lived "on the outside." I, too, was led astray by wrong thinking and by sin. But the good Lord summoned me back in. He showed me a world that I didn't know existed. Now, I'd like to show it to you.

This is a very personal invitation -- not from me, but from God Almighty. You are at this moment because He ordained it. You are reading these words because He chose you. He chose you to be a saint in eternal life. But it starts, right now, by rejecting death. By rejecting sin.

Listen: mortal sin is not a matter of debate. There IS right, and there IS wrong. There's no gray area here, friends. None. Ironically, though, one of the devil's greatest victories has been convincing the world that _all areas_ are gray areas. He's convinced many that there is no sin or virtue, life or death. He has blurred all definitive lines.

Friends, the devil did this for a very specific reason. He did it purposely. Because if all area is gray area (if all area is FOG), then you can't see the path! Life, then, is just aimless wandering... wandering to _sure death_. We are like meek, compliant sheep led to slaughter.

Look at the map!!! Please!! Look at where the gray area is on the map. It is OUTSIDE THE GATE. If, right now, all is "gray" in your world -- if all is acceptable and tolerable -- then you're in trouble. I'm sorry. But you are. Again, I am not judging you. I am simply concerned for you.

St. John Vianney told Maureen Sweeny Kyle in a recent apparition, "A person in sin, who dies suddenly without a chance for repentance, has _no chance for salvation_. The fact that sins are now culturally acceptable denies the necessity of being in a state of grace in order to achieve salvation... This topic of sin and of a state of grace must never be compromised to please man." (June 14, 2016)

The Bible, too, is clear that sin (and mortal sin) _do_ exist. 1 John 5:16 says, _"If anyone sees his brother sinning if the sin is not deadly, he should pray to God, and he will give him life. This is only for those whose sin is not deadly."_ Here in this passage, he's differentiating between two kinds of sin: mortal (deadly) and venial (non-deadly).

In Galatians 5, St. Paul lists several sins and then says, *"they which do such things shall not inherit the kingdom of God."*

He does it again in 1 Corinthians 6:9-10. *"They shall not inherit the kingdom of God."*

It really doesn't get much clearer than this. Sin is sin. And certain sins warrant the loss of eternal life. They merit death, damnation, hellfire. I know this is hard to hear, but it must be said. It must be accepted. Or there's really no use going any farther.

So, I guess the big question now is this: what are _mortal_ sins? What are _deadly_ sins? You might first think of the list, created by Pope Gregory the Great, called the "Seven Deadly Sins" (sometimes called the "Seven Capital Sins"). They are called 'deadly' because, yes, they *can* kill the life of grace in the soul. These are basically opposite the seven cardinal virtues.

1. Pride (which goes against the virtue of Humility)
2. Envy (which goes against the virtue of Kindness)
3. Gluttony (which goes against the virtue of Abstinence)
4. Lust (which goes against the virtue of Chastity)
5. Anger (which goes against the virtue of Patience)
6. Greed (which goes against the virtue of Liberality)
7. Sloth (which goes against the virtue of Diligence)

The "Seven Deadly Sins" are vices. But, they're _not_ necessarily mortal sins, in and of themselves.

Let me explain. The Seven Deadly Sins are the _basis_ of sin. They're what _causes_ sin. For example, a person with pride only sins when he _acts_ on that pride. So pride isn't necessarily the sin; it's the precursor to it. It's the thing that leads to sin.

If a prideful person is trying _not_ to act on this vice and actually resists action, then no real sin is committed. In fact, he may develop virtue instead by resisting. If his pride is strong, though, and he _does_ act, then yes, mortal sin can be committed, depending on the action.

So, what types of actions are considered mortal sins?

Mortal sin is any action (or inaction) that involves a serious matter, typically against one of the Ten Commandments, as the Catechism says (#1858). Mortal sin must also be committed with deliberate intent and full knowledge. What that means is, _"I used my free will to do this, and I knew it was wrong when I did it."_ You have to know it's wrong and choose it anyway. But understand: knowledge is not the same as belief.

If you have been informed that something is a mortal sin, but CHOOSE to believe it is not a mortal sin, then you DO have the knowledge, and you could be guilty as a result. If you truly do not know, though -- or do not choose the action -- it's not a mortal sin.

For example, a married woman who is raped by another man does not commit the sin of infidelity because the act took place against her free will. She didn't choose it. A Catholic child (baptized as an infant) who was never taken to church or taught anything about the faith does not sin against "keeping holy the Sabbath" because the inaction was without knowledge. He doesn't know he's Catholic, let alone what the Sabbath is.

When there _is_ knowledge and consent of free will, though, it is a completely different story. It is a mortal sin, then (if a serious matter), and it is deadly. Remember, this is not a matter of debate. The Blessed Mother told Maureen, "A Commandment cannot be negotiated just as each soul's judgment cannot be negotiated. A soul is either in a state of grace, or he is not." (April 14, 2016)

You see, when God gave us these Commandments, He did not just give us a "set of rules." He essentially put down gate posts to mark out boundary lines. These gate posts basically delineate where the almighty presence of God resides.

Yes, I know, God is omnipresent. So, you may be asking how God can be confined by boundary lines if He is supposedly everywhere. Well, here's the thing: God's Goodness, Life, Light, Protection, and Mercy are found within these boundaries. Outside these boundaries is where His Justice lives. That's where you experience His Wrath. (Although, as long as we are walking the earth, we still experience His mercy and goodness to some degree because He allows us to continue living. He allows us to have the opportunity to reenter the gate.)

So, the next question is: if mortal sin removes you from the garden (from grace), how the heck do you get back in?

It's simple: you need the Sacrament of Reconciliation (if you are Catholic) to return to a state of grace. If you are not Catholic, you still must repent in some way with a sincere and contrite heart.

Think of it like this: turning away from and rejecting sin is essentially turning away from and rejecting the dark area. When you confess a sin that you committed, you actually go back into the garden via that broken gate post by which you exited. When the priest raises his hand in the confessional and absolves you from your sin, what he is doing is reinstating you as a citizen in the Kingdom of God and in the garden of grace. You can't live there without this citizenship.

Through that priest, Jesus repairs the broken gate post. He heals you of the damage done by that sin. And friends, the annual, once-a-year confession at Christmas or Easter... yeah, I know that's the "requirement," but that's not going to get it done. I'm sorry.

We really should confess venial sins, too, which I'm certain most of us commit more than once a year. Venial sins are less severe sins. They are not deadly. They do not transport us out of the garden or remove us entirely from God's presence. But they do weaken grace in us. What's that mean? It means we are not as strong to resist mortal sin in the future. So, a person who frequently commits venial sin is _very_ likely to commit a mortal sin.

Saint Francis de Sales explains it this way in his book _The Introduction to the Devout Life_, "Spiders do not kill bees, but spoil and corrupt their honey and tangle honeycombs with their webs so that the bees cannot do their work... In like manner, venial sins do not kill the soul, but spoil its devotion and so entangle its powers and bad habits and inclinations so that it can no longer exert a prompt charity that constitutes devotion."

What frequent confession does is strengthen your conscience. It anchors the garden gate into a firm foundation to keep you from wandering outside. Venial sin loosens the gate posts, so to speak. Constant venial sin can loosen the posts to such a degree that an opening is created.... an opening through which demons come to tempt you and through which you slip out into mortal sin. The frequency of your confession, therefore, is basically the strength of your gate.

Some of you may still be doubting the seriousness of repentance and Reconciliation. May I remind you what Jesus said in Scripture, *"I tell you again: unless you repent you will also perish."* (Luke 13:3)

The Sacrament of Reconciliation is imperative for a successful journey. As Jesus said to Maureen, "...the soul whose faults are revealed to him is being called to conversion and into the First Chamber... It is only his _repentance_ that allows him to pass through the door... Then the soul is cooperating with the grace that is being given, and My Victory is beginning in him." (November 28, 2003)

So, when was the last time you went to confession? Ideally, we should take advantage of this great gift once a month... every two weeks, even. And it should not be taken lightly. A sincere examination of conscience should be done before making a good confession. We should take time to reflect on the Ten Commandments, which spells out mortal sin.

Since the goal of this book is to ENTER the garden and actually take the journey (not just learn about it), we will do this examination of conscience right here, right now. There's no time like the present.

As you read, make a mental note of your failings (or even write them down), both mortal and venial. Afterward, I hope you will make an appointment with a priest to confess these in the Sacrament of Reconciliation (if you are Catholic). You can also just go during the regularly scheduled Confession times, which are usually listed in a parish bulletin. Most bulletins are on the parish website too. If you have not been to confession in a very long time, there will be a section at the end of this chapter called "What to Expect," which will guide you through the process.

If you are _not_ Catholic, I advise finding a pastor or friend, some type of confidant that you trust. Speak your confession and repentance in the presence of a witness, asking them to pray for you and with you. Make it ceremonial. Make an event out of it. Show God you are serious about this, and you desire to be reinstated in the garden.

Do not be nervous, though. Be excited! Understand that we are all sinners, and we all need to do this. Understand you are the prodigal son (in Luke 15:11-32), and the Lord awaits you with great anticipation and immense love. Remember: He is the Almighty one. No sin of yours is greater than His love.

Now let's get started...

The First Commandment:

"Do not worship other gods besides Me." God says, "I am a jealous God who will not share your affection with any other god...those who hate Me I punish the children for the sins of their parents to the third and fourth generation...But I lavish My love on those who love Me and obey My commands, even for one thousand generations." (Ex. 20:16)

1. Have I participated in anything of the occult? This includes fortune tellers, horoscope readings, Ouija boards, even forms of yoga.

2. Do I exalt anything in my life above God? This includes my body, senses, money, and reputation.

The Second Commandment:

"Do not misuse the name of the Lord your God. The Lord will not let you go unpunished if you misuse His name." (Exodus 20:7)

1. Have I cried out "God!" or "Jesus Christ!" in a manner other than prayer? This includes the phrase, "Oh my God."

The Third Commandment:

"Keep holy the Sabbath. Six days a week are set apart for your daily duties and regular work, but the seventh day is a day of rest dedicated to the Lord your God..." (Exodus 21:8)

2. Have I missed Mass on a Sunday or any Holy Day of Obligation?
3. Have I worked on Sunday, doing duties that could be saved for another time?

The Fourth Commandment:

"Honor your father and your mother. Then you will live a long full life in the land that Lord will give you." (Ex. 21:12)

1. Do I show kindness and respect to my parents in my words and actions?
2. Does my behavior in public bring honor or dishonor to my parents and our family name?
3. Do I forgive my parents for their wrongdoing, or do I hold grudges against them?

4. Do I pray for my parents every day (whether living or deceased)?

The Fifth Commandment:

"You shall not murder" (Exodus 20:13)

1. Have I caused, supported, or participated in the unnatural death of another human person? This includes euthanasia, suicide, abortion, and the use of some birth control pills, which are actually abortifacient drugs.
2. Have I caused, supported, or participated in a loss of spiritual life in another person by promoting heresy and error and coercing them away from the truths of the Church?
3. Have I caused, supported, or participated in killing the spirit (the joy or peace) of another person by bullying or attacking them?
4. Have I caused, supported, or participated in killing the reputation of another person through gossip, slander, or detraction?

The Sixth Commandment:

"Do not commit adultery." (Exodus 20:14)

1. Am I a married person who has had sexual contact with someone other than my spouse? (This includes flirting, dating, or any intimate touching.)
2. Am I a single person who has had sex outside the marriage covenant?
3. Have I committed the sin of masturbation?

4. Have I purposely lusted over someone through the use of pornography?
5. Have I caused someone to lust over me by purposely wearing revealing clothes?

The Seventh Commandment:

"Do not steal." (Exodus 20:15)

1. Have I taken, without permission, any material thing from anyone at any time?
2. Have I unjustly cut wages—or withhold raises—from hard-working, deserving employees?
3. Have I failed to give to others that which I am obligated to give? This includes tithing to my church and giving to the poor.
4. Do I "steal the thunder" of others by withholding praise or kind words towards my neighbor?
5. Have I stolen the innocence from any child through my words, actions, or choices in entertainment?

The Eighth Commandment:

"You shall not bear dishonest witness against your neighbor."
(Exodus 20:16)

1. Have I told an untruth (no matter how slight) about my neighbor, and how often have I told it?
2. Have I allowed an untruth to spread by refusing to oppose it with truth?
3. Have I acted with a hidden agenda or ulterior motive towards anyone in any area of life?
4. Have I embraced false, anti-Christian principles in the church or in society?

The Ninth Commandment:

"You shall not covet your neighbor's wife." (Exodus 20:17)

1. Have I entertained sinful acts in my thoughts through fantasy and day-dreaming?
2. Do I look at others - in public or on television - in an impure way?
3. Am I completely faithful to my spouse or significant other in my thoughts and heart?

The Tenth Commandment:

"You shall not covet... anything that belongs to your neighbor." (Exodus 20:17)

1. Am I jealous or envious of any material or spiritual thing that my neighbor has?
2. Am I unsatisfied with my life to the point that I cannot see or appreciate the many blessings God has bestowed upon me?

What to Expect in the Sacrament of Reconciliation:

Below is a step by step outline of the Sacrament of Reconciliation. If you are nervous, remember GAC-PAD: Greeting, Admittance, Confession - Penance, Absolution, and Dismissal. If you forget when you get into the confessional, feel free to ask the priest for help. And rest assured: it will not be the first time he has been asked this.

Step 1 -- Greeting: The priest welcomes you to the sacrament.

Step 2 --Admittance: Tell the priest you have sinned, and also state how long it has been since you have confessed. You may say something like, "Bless me, Father. I have sinned. It has been _______ since my last confession."

Step 3 -- Confession: The priest may acknowledge the admittance and then ask you what your sins are. You then list/confesses the specific sins you have committed.

Step 4 -- Penance (and Counsel): The priest may offer counsel regarding the sins you confessed and ask you to pray or do something as penance to make up for and atone for the sins you just confessed.

Step 5 -- Absolution: The priest then prays the Prayer of Absolution, to which the penitent responds: "Amen," and you make the sign of the Cross.

Step 6 -- Dismissal: You are then free to leave the confessional.

Chapter Four: The Door of Mary

"Many fail to discover the path of salvation and fall prey to Satan's deceit. Therefore, I have sent My Mother ahead of Me with the message of Holy Love. I have come after Her, revealing the message of Divine Love and the complete message of Our United Hearts."

~Jesus to Maureen, January 24, 2001

Once you've made a good confession and confessed any mortal sin, you're reinstated to citizenship in the garden. How exciting! Congratulations! But, now what?

Well, if you look at the map (the garden image on the cover of this book), the first thing you see at the center of the gate is the Blessed Virgin Mary. Mary is the first "chamber" in the United Hearts diagram shown to Maureen also. (See left.)

The Chambers of the United Hearts as shown to Maureen Sweeney-Kyle at Holy Love Ministries.

So, we're going to start with Her because, well, that's where Jesus wants us to start.

Jesus was very clear about this in a message

He gave to Maureen. "The First chamber of My Heart is the Immaculate Heart of My Holy Mother, Mary ...no one can come to Me except through Her Heart..." (April 7, 2000)

I know there's a lot of people out there -- Protestant friends and even Catholic friends -- who don't like to talk about Mary. They don't think Mary has anything to do with their spiritual journey. According to them, they don't "need" Mary to get to Jesus. They just go to Him directly. If you're one of these people who think this way, you may now be tempted to close up this book and quit the retreat. I ask you not to do that. Please. Do not be afraid of this chapter. Please. I beg you. Just give me a few minutes. I'm going to try to clear up this confusion right now.

Okay, here's the thing. Jesus said, *"Follow Me,"* right? He came to *"show us the way"* to the Father, right? Well, friends, listen: <u>He</u> chose to come to us through the doorway of Mary, and He expects us to return to Him via that same doorway. He entered the physical world through Her in order to get to us, and we are to enter the spiritual world through Her in order to get back to Him.

Now, I have to say something here that might sound harsh to some. But I told you in the last chapter I'm not tip-toeing around the garden. So here goes. This mentality that we don't "need" Mary... well, it has its roots in pride.

In fact, this mentality is quite similar to Lucifer's mentality when he fell from Heaven. That's how serious it is. God revealed his plan to Lucifer (that he was to assist and guard the human race), but Lucifer said, "I will not serve." As an angel of light, he felt there was a better, loftier plan for him than assisting little humans. He could not humble himself and consent to the plan.

So, all light and grace were removed from him on account of his disobedience, and he became an angel of darkness, the devil.

Likewise, those who are adamantly and defiantly against the role of Blessed Virgin Mary have a hard time humbling themselves and consenting to the plan. They feel there is a better, loftier plan, like going directly to Jesus. The problem is, they are losing out on grace and depriving themselves of light.

Now, am I saying these people are evil, like the devil, just because they don't like Mary? Absolutely NOT. No, no, no. Some of these people are very, VERY devout Christians who love the Lord deeply. What I'm saying is that, while they _do_ have a great deal of light and grace, they could still have more.

The fact of the matter is, they are missing a crucial component to the journey. Jesus confirms this in a message He gave to Maureen. "Some souls lie permanently vanquished at the threshold, giving in to the pride of disbelief. Others see the spiritual benefit they are being offered. They pick up the key to the Chamber of Holy Love, which is the title and ejaculatory prayer, 'Mary, Protectress of the Faith and Refuge of Holy Love, come to my aid.' Thus they are admitted and led deeper into the Chambers of Our United Hearts." (February 10, 2006)

Jesus did not come directly to us, so we cannot go directly to Him. He _could_ have come directly to us, yes. But He didn't. So we are to do what He did. We are to go through Her. We can take no other way than the way He Himself took. That's reason number one, why we start with Mary.

Reason number two is: _"Hail Mary, full of grace."_ (Luke 1:28) If you want to enter a state of grace (the garden of grace), you're going to have to do it via the "Dispenser of Grace." And I'm sorry to tell you; _we_ don't get to determine who that "Dispenser" is. There's only one person who assigns that role or employs that position, and that's God. And He chose the Blessed Mother Mary.

I'm not going to get into the theology of Mary as "Mediatrix of all Grace," but know that it is out there and that it's true. Saints and Pope's have written about it extensively for decades. So, if you feel led, you can find the information on it easily if you search.

St. Bernardine of Siena put it quite simply: "Every grace granted to man has three degrees in order; for by God it is communicated to Christ, from Christ it passes to the Virgin, and from the Virgin, it descends to us."

And for the people who happen to disagree with that pipeline, still complaining about going through Mary... well, listen, we've got to get over ourselves. Really. I mean, let's say tomorrow I decided to march into the Oval Office to speak to the President. What if I said, _"I'm an American citizen too. I don't need to go through secretaries or advisors. I'm just going directly to him for what I need."_

I _hope_ one of you would care enough about me and have the guts to tell me, _"Uh, Stace, yeah, you actually _do_ need to go through them because that's just how it works."_ Friends, this is me, caring enough about you to tell you: you actually _do_ need to go through Mary. That's just how it works. Okay?

Now, reason number four, why we start with Mary: Mary is the Protectress of our Faith. She's protecting and guarding the garden. This ties into a couple of different things. One, look at the stream of Living Water on the map. It proceeds from the

Tree of Life. Mary is at the mouth of the Stream, right? That is because Mary is espoused to the Holy Spirit. If God said that in a human marriage, "the two become one" (Mark 10:8, Genesis 2:24, and Ephesians 5:31), would He not do the same when He takes His Own Spouse? Of course. Mary is ONE with the Holy Spirit.

The Bible says the Spirit came upon Her and overshadowed Her. Her job then is His job. Espoused, they work together. The Spirit is called the Guardian of the Faith. So Mary is the Protectress of the Faith. She is the Protectress of the garden, where our faith is formed.

Listen, it's just like when you pray to the Father, you pray through Jesus because there's no separation in the Trinity. Jesus said, *"the Father and I are one."* (John 17:21) You might be *focused* on one person in the Trinity when you pray, but that doesn't make the other Persons less present or less attentive to your prayer. So it is with Mary.

Friends, when we live "in the Spirit," we live in Mary. When we pray "in the Spirit," we pray through Mary. And I said pray *through* Mary, not *to* Mary. The rumor that Catholics pray *to* Mary is preposterous. All prayer is directed to God alone. I'm talking about praying with Mary in the Holy Spirit. Think of it as your own little, internal prayer group with influential "insiders."

Another reason why She is our Protectress is because she is the Mother of the Church, the mother of each one of us. Jesus gave Her to us from the Cross when He said, *"Behold thy Mother."* (John 19:27) You might ask what that has to do with being our Protectress? Well, have you ever crossed a Momma bear in the woods?? Have you ever tried to touch a bear cub with the

Momma nearby? Yeah, ok, then you get it. Momma's are protectors. Period. End of story.

But there's even more to it. Her protection was foretold in the very beginning in the Garden of Eden when God told the serpent, "I will put enmity between you and the Woman, and between your offspring and Hers. She will crush thy head while you strike at Her heel." (Genesis 3:15)

God Himself placed _enmity_ between them -- between Mary and the devil. God is the one who involved Mary in this great battle. Would He have made them enemies and then not equipped Mary to do battle? Of course not. That's just mean. He put them in total, mutual opposition of each other and gave Her power against Him. Because Eve listened to the serpent in the garden and coerced Adam into sin, the New Eve (Mary) will crush the serpent in the spiritual garden and protect men from sin. She was given this power from God Himself. He ordained it at the very beginning.

Jesus confirmed this in a message to Maureen, "When you feel your feet slip from the path, you doubt or fear, call on My Mother PROTECTRESS of the FAITH, and She will restore your faith. She will place your feet firmly back upon the path of righteousness." (August 12, 2002)

Later, He added, "...invoke [Mary] 'Protectress of the Faith' in the face of any temptation or doubt. Instantly evil will flee, and peace will be restored to the troubled heart." (January 21, 2010)

Again, we don't have time to get into the nitty-gritty on the theology of her protection (there are whole books written just on this topic). You can research it on your own, though, if you feel led to. There are countless real-life, undeniable stories illustrating her protection also --- through the miraculous medal, the rosary, Her images. Time and time again, She comes to the aid of Her children who need Her.

OK, now, reason number five why we start with Mary: Mary is united with Jesus. I know some people might be thinking, *"What?? Hold the phone! You can't say that!"* I've actually had people (Catholics) totally freak out at me when I say this. But, wait just a minute, and listen. I did not say *"equal to Jesus."* I said, *"united to Jesus."* There's a big, gigantic difference. No one is equal to God, but we are *all* (every single last one of us) called to union with Him.

The only thing that separates us from God is sin and a failure to conform to God's will. Since Mary was sinless, she complied perfectly with His will. So, She is perfectly united to Him.

Some, I know, disagree that Mary was sinless. But listen, Mary is the new Ark of the New Covenant. In the Old Testament, the Ark had to be pure and untouched by sinful man. In 2 Samuel 6:6-7, it says, "Uzzah stretched out his hand to the ark of God and...God struck him on that spot, and he died there in God's presence." If the old Ark could not have a trace of sin touch it, how then can we possibly think that God would come to dwell in a womb (the new Ark) of a sinful woman? It is not logical.

The fact is, Mary was saved by God like the rest of us -- She was just saved in a different manner. The Franciscan theologian Duns Scotus explained it this way: falling into sin is like a man falling into a deep ditch. The man would need someone to lower a rope and save him. But if someone were to warn him of the pit ahead of time, preventing him from falling into it, he would still be saved. Likewise, Mary was saved from sin by receiving the grace that prevented Her from falling into it. But she was still saved.

Because of this great grace, and because she was sinless, she was perfectly united with Jesus. Saint John Paul the Great spoke about the United Hearts of Jesus and Mary in great detail over the course of his papacy. Many other saints did, too, including St. Louis De Montfort, St. Bonaventure, and St. Maximilian Kobe. Jesus and Mary themselves have even spoken about it to visionaries and mystics like Sister Lucy Santos of Fatima, the seers in Medegorjie, and now Maureen Sweeney Kyle in Ohio.

The fact is, Mary is the door -- the entryway -- of the garden that leads to the Kingdom of God. She is the first chamber of the United Hearts (which leads to the Hearts of Jesus and the Eternal Father).

She's like the Foyer of God's house. When you're in the foyer, you're not really "inside" yet, but you've crossed the threshold. You're under the roof, so to speak. You're safe from the "outside" elements. This is why Jesus and Mary have continuously told Maureen that the first chamber is "salvation."

Now, if we said that you enter the garden through prayer and recollection, and we also said Mary is the beginning or the entryway... then what _kind_ of prayer is likely to be the most effective in helping us enter? Yep, Marian prayer.

It can be as simple as, *"Mary, Protectress of the Faith, come to my aid."* Jesus stressed the importance of this particular prayer in a message He gave to Maureen on October 16, 2000. He said, "This simple prayer admits the soul into the first Chamber...which is the Immaculate Heart of Mary. With faith protected and Satan laid waste, the soul opens his heart to...the First Chamber of the United Hearts."

With this prayer, She protects you and draws you in. She takes you deep into the mysteries of God, deep into the Spiritual garden, deep into the Most Holy Trinity. Another beloved Marian prayer is the rosary.

Jesus told Maureen, " I, your Jesus, love the prayer of the Mass the most. Then I love the Rosary." (April 24, 1999)

Now, you're absolutely right. You don't _have_ to do it this way. You don't _have_ to pray the rosary or invoke the Blessed Mother's assistance or protection. You're right. Marian prayer is _not_ a requirement for anyone. But, I'm going to tell you: it is the fastest, more-assured way. If you don't believe me, try it and prove me wrong. I double-dog dare you! :) I could write books on the number of ways the Blessed Mother has helped me and worked miracles in my life, most often through the rosary.

And, friends, even if you choose _not_ to invoke Mary -- if you just don't think you can take that drastic step -- it doesn't change the absolute truth that Mary is involved in your spiritual journey. The Blessed Mother is constantly shedding grace on Her children. She is constantly drawing them out of the darkness and imploring Her spouse on their behalf so that they may be moved interiorly to enter the garden. Even if those children want absolutely nothing to do with Her.

Listen, it is _grace_ (and grace alone!)that moves a soul to remorse. It is grace that draws a soul to the confessional—nothing else. If you were moved to repentance in the last chapter, then that, my friend, was a grace bestowed on you through the hands of the Blessed Virgin Mary. We don't have remorse in us, naturally, on our own, because the flesh is carnal and faulty. It's a _grace_ given to us from the hands of Mary, who is "full of grace."

Do you see the gate posts on the map? Do you see the image on each one? It is a picture of the Immaculate Heart of Mary. The Mother of Pearl is inscribed on the "pearly gates." The Mother of the Church is inscribed on the 24 garden gate posts surrounding the New Jerusalem -- which represent the 12 tribes of Israel and the 12 apostles, through which this church came about.

Her image on the gate posts signifies not only her protection but also the grace she provides in order to keep us within the "city limits," so to speak. The gate is sort of an extension of the door. For it is grace that cements these posts into the soil of your faith.

So here we are at another pivotal place in the journey. We stand in the doorway. Satan lays siege upon our hearts in the hopes that we will doubt, abandon this message, and run from the foyer.

Jesus told Maureen, "...the most important step in personal holiness lies at the threshold of entry into the First Chamber-- the Immaculate Heart of Mary... It is upon this threshold the soul is engaged in the greatest spiritual warfare. It is at the entrance of My Mother's Heart that the soul decides to believe or disbelieve..." (February 10, 2006)

So, here we are, with a choice to make. Perhaps a difficult one. Perhaps you've never considered Mary before. Perhaps this message even goes against everything you've ever been taught.

But, my friend, you are being called. Summoned. I ask you to open your heart to the invitation.

Hear, deep in your heart, the words of Jesus spoken to Maureen, "I urge you in your greatest fears which the enemy puts in your hearts, invoke the Name of My Mother 'Mary Protectress of the Faith'... for it is Satan who draws you into fear. It is I who call you to trust. Satan flees before this Title of My Most Holy Mother. Remember It. Use It!" (October 26, 2001)

Do you hear Him? Do you feel Him? Speak the following words (out loud if possible), "Mary, Protectress of the Faith, come to my aid."

Set your doubts aside. Lay your uncertainties behind you. Place your hand upon the doorknob and turn. Move forward, my friend. A garden paradise awaits you. I look forward to seeing you in the next chapter.

Meditation

"Again, I say, sit with your Mother during this time. I will bless you, abundantly. It is by Her intercession that you have been given the Spirit of Wisdom and Knowledge. She implored Her Spouse on your behalf. Sit with Her, child. Let your Mother teach you about the passion, death, and resurrection of Jesus, Her Son. You ask to know it more intimately. By Her side, I shall grant your request. You will not have the strength to bear this knowledge apart from the Fount of Grace. Remember, She is always with Me. When you sit with Her, you sit with Me. I am there. Many of your blessings you owe to Her. She pleads to Me for you. Oh, how She loves you. It is my great joy to provide for the Woman who bore My only begotten Son, who willingly offered Him for My Will and My Glory. We cannot resist Her requests. The day begins. Keep wait with your Mother. Your company eases Her sorrow. I am with you in this." *(An excerpt from "Mornings with my Father" by Stacy Mal.)*

Prayer

Mary, Protectress of the Faith, come to my aid. Defend me in the attacks of the enemy. Implore your Spouse, the Holy Spirit, on my behalf that I may receive greater wisdom and knowledge regarding you, my Mother, and the Mother of the Most High God, Jesus Christ. Give me the grace to enter this first chamber with confidence and trust. In Jesus' Name, I pray. Amen.

Scripture

"In the sixth month, the angel Gabriel was sent from God to a town of Galilee called Nazareth, to a virgin betrothed to a man named Joseph, of the house of David, and the virgin's name was Mary. And coming to her, he said, 'Hail, full of grace, the Lord is with you.' But she was greatly troubled at what was said and pondered what sort of greeting this might be. Then the angel said to her, 'Do not be afraid, Mary, for you have found favor with God. Behold, you will conceive in your womb and bear a son, and you shall name him Jesus. He will be great and will be called Son of the Most High, and the Lord God will give him the throne of David, his father, and he will rule over the house of Jacob forever, and of his kingdom, there will be no end.' But

Mary said to the angel, 'How can this be since I have no relations with a man?' And the angel said to her in reply, 'The Holy Spirit will come upon you, and the power of the Most High will overshadow you. Therefore the child to be born will be called holy, the Son of God.'" (Luke 1:26-35)

Questions for Reflection

What aspects regarding the theology of Mary mentioned in this chapter do you struggle with most? Ask now for the grace to overcome these struggles. Sincerely desire to understand Mary's role in the spiritual journey.

What aspects of the theology of Mary do you *like* the best and why? Mary, as the Dispenser of Grace? Our Protectress? The Door/Entryway to Jesus? The enemy of the Devil?

Consider the vocation of motherhood. Think about a woman you know who is a very good mother. What qualities do you admire in her? What specific virtues make her a good mother?

Envision the Blessed Virgin Mary as the best and most admirable mother -- your mother. What type of assistance or "mothering" could you use in your life right now? Ask Her for this assistance and be open to "seeing" Her work in your life.

Chapter Five: The Weeds

"The holy person has entered the First Chamber—the Immaculate Heart of Mary. He hungers for God but has many areas of self-love still in his heart. One trap that Satan lays for such a one is the soul's desire to be known as holy. Of course, each soul in the First Chamber has unique temptations. He should pray every day that they be shown to him. Only in this way can he be perfected."

~ St. Thomas Aquinas to Maureen, December 9, 2005

Well, I'm glad to see you are starting this chapter and that you kept going through the door. I'm glad to see you have chosen to enter the first level or chamber.

The first level is an extension of the door... kind of like how a foyer or entryway is an extension of a door. This first chamber is the Foyer of Mary. Since Mary is sinless, this foyer is pure white. Since she is espoused to the Holy Spirit, it is pure light. So, when we first enter the foyer from the outer area, we come in like dirty children who have been playing rambunctiously outside. We come in from darkness into a bright, clean, stark-white room, and we can't help but notice our filth in comparison.

Now, if we look at the map, you will see that the first level inside the gate is a level of weeds and tall grass. These represent our biggest faults and failings. Weeds, as we know, are not only eyesores in a garden (like glaring faults are eyesores to the soul), they also threaten the health and life of the garden too (like sin threatens the health and life of the soul).

The weeds represent big, ugly grass stains on the soul when it enters the foyer. Inside this first chamber, we become keenly aware of these, and we receive the grace to want to get rid of them.

Jesus describes this to Maureen, "In the First Chamber, the soul is illuminated through the Flame of My Mother's Heart to see his soul as it stands before Me. His most glaring faults are brought to light in this Flame, and he is given the grace of wanting to change." (May 30, 2014)

Here, in this first level, we receive self-knowledge. We become intensely aware of our most glaring faults, through Mary, in the Light of the Holy Spirit. Surrounded by pure holiness, we realize we are _not_ holy.

At this point, we have two choices. One, we can hate the white, clean surroundings and rush back outside. Here's where many people begin to complain about Christianity, or religion in general. They're standing in this white foyer, they know they're dirty, and they say, *"don't judge me. I'm a good person. The Church just condemns people."* And so forth and so on. (Ohhhhhh, boy, was that me in my early 20s.)

Jesus described these souls to Maureen, "...there are those who hear Her call and believe, but spurn the invitation along with the unbelievers. The numbers of those who are invited, but will not respond, are far above those who accept the invitation. Indeed, the threshold to the First Chamber is the most decisive in the entire spiritual journey." (September 4, 2000)

Instead of hating the stains, these souls hate the light that reveals them. And so they leave. They start saying things like, *"I'm spiritual, not religious."* They don't want anything to do with anything that's going to hold them accountable or point out any flaw within them. They have no interest in becoming better; they simply want to be comfortable.

It's like John 3:20, which says, *"For everyone who does wicked things hates the light and does not come toward the light so that his works might not be exposed."*

Jesus described it further, "The moment a soul hears the call to conversion of heart, he stands at the threshold of the first Chamber... My Mother meets the souls who stand precariously on this threshold of conversion and salvation. She extends to them every grace they need to accept Her invitation to enter the first portal of Our United Hearts. She weeps for those who turn away. With a Mother's Heart, She calls them back over and over." (September 4, 2000)

Turning away from the journey is simply a lack of humility. So, please understand how important humility is and how deadly pride is. Humility is the foundational virtue in this whole journey. Without it, you're not going anywhere, whether you have the map or not. You don't have a fighting chance in this garden without humility. So, begin to pray for it now, and earnestly desire it.

St Teresa of Avila said, *"Nothing matters more ... than humility. Begin by entering the room where humility is acquired rather than by flying off to the other rooms. For that is the way to make progress..."*

Our second option (instead of rushing back outside to the outer area) is to embrace humility and say "yes" as Mary did at the Annunciation. We say yes to the journey, yes to "cleaning ourselves up." We say yes to the first level of the garden and the work it will require. We see the stains -- we see our obvious faults -- and we agree to let the Holy Spirit (the Living Water) bathe us.

This is what theologians call the stage of purification. Here's where Mary, the Dispenser of Grace, sheds grace on your soul so that you have the ability to see the bad habits that you're going to need to prune, cut back, and dig up. Here's where the dirty child in the spotless foyer actually gets cleaned up in order to move deeper into the Heart of God.

Let me explain it another way. When you first reenter the garden, you experience life and growth in your soul. And this is good. It's better than darkness and death, of course. The gray area is like a rocky, barren ground where nothing grows. But in the beginning, this "life and growth" is mostly weeds. It reveals that the garden of the soul has been unkempt and unattended for quite some time, and now there are weeds of bad habits and unhealthy desires growing wild in there.

This is probably one of the most difficult stages. One, it's closest to the outer area, so even though you're saved, and you're inside the gate, you're still close enough to hear the demons yelling at you... tempting you, trying to trick you and coerce you into leaving.

Jesus explained it to Maureen like this, "The first door the soul must open is perhaps the most difficult. Through the Flame of My Mother's Heart, the soul recognizes its faults and failings. By a movement of free will, he decides to overcome his weaknesses... It is the purgative stage. The soul may open this door, quite committed to the path he sees before him, but because he gives in to Satan's temptations, he finds himself outside the first door again. Over and over he may have to re-commit..." (October 16, 1999)

St. Teresa of Avila also talked about this stage in her book *Interior Castle* (though again, she referred to these as "rooms" in the interior castle, not chambers or levels). She said, "The devil has many legions of evil spirits in each room to prevent souls from passing from one to another," she says. "And as we, poor souls, fail to realize this, we are tricked by all kinds of deception. The devil is less successful with those who are near the King's dwelling place (in the center of the garden), but at this early stage, as the soul is still absorbed in worldly affairs, engulfed in worldly pleasure and puffed up with worldly honors and ambitions... such a soul is easily vanquished."

So you see, it's not uncommon for souls in this stage to give in to these temptations, to fall back into the dark, outer area, having to reenter the confessional time and time again. But don't lose heart!! Go to the confessional as often as it takes. This is how you overcome!

Another reason why it's the most difficult stage is because it often takes the most work. Some of these weeds, like pride, have very deep roots. They've been growing deep in the soil of your heart for quite some time, and they are not going to be removed easily. Some of these -- like unforgiveness -- have been growing unchecked and have taken over a great deal of space in the garden of the soul. They've reached out into all kinds of areas of life -- other relationships, etc. Again, it's not going to be easy to clear these out. But it absolutely must be done.

St. Thomas Aquinas explained it to Maureen this way, "Spiritual pride is deadly. It is like trying to reach a destination blindfolded, refusing to be led or to remove the blindfold because the soul presumes he knows his way. Everything about trustful surrender, which embraces this message has to do with free will. If through spiritual pride the soul thinks he is in the right place spiritually, he will not move his will to enter the First Chamber...'" (September 10, 2001)

Here, you're going to have to look at yourself -- in prayer and recollection (with Mary, in the Holy Spirit) -- and you're going to have to admit, *"I'm impatient. I have a lot of pride. I am jealous or unforgiving,"* or whatever the weeds are. And friends, you're going to have to work on it. You're going to have to *do* something about it. Here's why I said it's not enough to talk about the garden or look at or just learn about it. You cannot pursue holiness -- or make the spiritual journey -- in your intellect.

The garden isn't in your head. It's in your heart.

And you can't be hasty!! In his book, *Introduction to the Devout Life*, St Francis de Sales said, "The beginning of good health is to be purged of our sinful tendencies. The usual purgation and healing, whether of body or soul, takes place only little by little, and by passing from one advance to another with difficulty and patience."

So, you can't just say, *"oh, there's a weed of jealousy,"* and then casually say to yourself, *"I'll just stop being jealous."* No. That's like just snapping off the weed from the surface. You left the root intact. No. You have to sit with that weed in prayer, and you have to ask for greater self-knowledge regarding the <u>root</u> of that jealousy. Is it an insecurity within you? An uncared-for wound, or a hidden unforgiveness? What is it? You have to ask yourself: what caused that to grow inside of me?

When you receive the grace to understand the depth of the root -- and the type of root this weed has -- you will know better how to uproot it and get rid of it. Some roots grow deep, straight down in the heart. Some grow wide. They reach out and affect other areas of our spiritual life. Don't assume you know how to pull it up unless you've taken it to prayer and recollection. Roots are hidden from our view. Ask the Blessed Mother for the grace to understand it and the strength to uproot it if you truly want to be rid of it and move forward.

Another thing we must consider is that these weeds didn't just magically appear in the garden. We planted each one ourselves. That weed took root in us because we fed it and watered it with an *affection* we have for that particular sin. Meaning, we enjoyed it or liked it -- to some degree -- or we wouldn't have chosen it or continued to let it grow.

Some people enjoy making fun of others or gossiping. Some people enjoy excessive drinking or parties. Some married people enjoy flirting. Some people enjoy social media while neglecting duties. The list goes on and on. We need to face the fact that there's often something about a sin that we enjoy. Otherwise, we wouldn't commit it.

So, please understand: it's not enough to pull the weeds. It's not even enough to dig up their roots. We have to get rid of the *affection* for these as well. Now, how on earth do you do that?? How in the world do you get your carnal self to stop liking something your spiritual self knows is bad?

St. Francis de Sales says to begin to see sins as enemies --- an enemy who, "if you give in to his courting, will surely destroy you."

Imagine there was a person who caused you great harm. Say he or she secretly poured gasoline on you while you slept and then lured you to a bonfire with friends. Say she put some horrid chemicals in the drink she prepared for you, knowing these chemicals would eat away at your flesh, starting first with your vital organs. Or say she constantly stole from you until you were left with nothing -- no food, clothing, or even home.

If you did not know the things this person did to you in secret, you might continue a friendship with him or her. But once you discover this "real friend" and all that he or she has done to destroy you, chances are you might develop an aversion, even a real hatred towards this person. You would vow to cut him or her out of your life, to protect yourself, and you would no doubt keep that vow, I'm sure.

Friends, in order to purge your carnal nature from an _affection_ for sin, we MUST begin to see sin as this so-called friend. This enemy. We must see it as a relationship that, on the surface, seems harmless, even pleasurable -- but secretly destroys you, disfigures you from the image and likeness of God, eats away at the life of grace inside you, and robs you of your inheritance, your home in Heaven.

In order to purge yourself from the affection of sin, you must begin to see sin in its ugly truth. Give it a name even, a persona. Allow aversion toward it to grow and develop into hatred. Then cut it out of your life. Never to look back on that sin again. Do not be like Lot's wife, though, who looked back on the sinful city she was fleeing. God turned her into a pillar of salt immediately.

(Genesis 19:26) Likewise, you will experience death if you look back at that sin.

Here at this level, we must force ourselves first to look at the root of sin so that we never have to look at the actual sin again. So often, our focus gets stuck on the good that we do in life, and our grave faults fly under our radar. It's as if we give charity a megaphone so as to drown out the failure. But what is actually happening behind the scenes is that the failure is killing the charity. We call attention to a flower on a weed as if it is a good thing. But this type of flower bears no fruit. In fact, the weed is choking out the fruit.

St. Francis de Sales explains it this way, "A man given to fasting thinks himself very devout if he fasts, although his heart may be filled with hatred. Much concerned with sobriety, he doesn't wet his tongue with wine or even water but won't hesitate to drink of his neighbor's blood by detraction."

He continued by saying, "Many persons clothe themselves with certain outward actions connected with holy devotion, and believe that they are truly devout and spiritual, but they are in fact nothing but copies and phantoms of devotion."

Therefore, to make any real progress in the spiritual life, we must begin to address the weeds. But please understand how important it is to take all this to prayer. Allow the Living Water of God to bathe you in the foyer of Mary, and clean the grass stains. Begin to pull up the weeds that caused these stains. Pull them up by the roots. But remember, roots are hidden from us. They are known only to the Eternal Gardener who sees all in truth -- and to the Woman, Mary, who He has employed in this work.

So we must enter prayer first. There, we must be instructed and taught about the nature of these weeds. Please, friends, do not underestimate how productive this can be. I have done it myself and can testify to how powerful it is.

In fact, the below meditation is an excerpt from my prayer journal. It is something that God spoke to my heart one morning years ago when I was in the garden, working on some "grass stains." Actually, that particular day He showed me a dirty, crusty skillet. I knew it was me. I knew the skillet was my soul. And you have to know: I hate pots and pans. Hate them. I'm notorious for letting dinner pans soak -- sometimes for days -- because I hate them so bad. I'm not proud of it, but it's true. It's so much easier to scrub them after they soak, you know? Well, during prayer, in the garden, God revealed my dirt and then asked _me_ to soak in Him. He's asking the same of you today.

Meditation

My child, come to me as often as you can. Not just in these pages. Come to me in the depths of your heart. Read what I have said to you in the past and sit in my presence. Soak in my Spirit. There is still much work to be done on you and with you. There are areas I still must scrub and clean for you to fully become a new creation... in order for you to be used in my handiwork. But first, child, soak. You must be clean to be used for my glory, or your stain will taint and spoil the flavor of my work. Soak. These spots are the toughest. They have been here the longest. Soak. The scrubbing will be difficult and most painful for you if you do not use this time. Sit still in my presence... in the Living Water of your God. Let my warmth soften what is hardened. Let me loosen what is fixed to you. Let me detach you, child, from the dirt. If you soak, the process of purification is much easier. Keep this word at the front of your mind. Keep this in your heart as I show you the areas that need tending. Do not get discouraged. Soak. It is much quicker this way. Be at peace, my child. *(An excerpt from "Mornings with my Father" by Stacy Mal.)*

Prayer

Mary, Protectress of the Faith, come to my aid. Shed grace on my soul that I may see the weeds threatening me. Use these moments of prayer -- and all the events of today -- to reveal them to me. Come, Holy Spirit, Living Water of God. Surround me. Fill Me. Let me rest in you, soak in you. Carry me in Your current of Divine Will, through the garden of grace. Cleanse me. Wash me. Renew me—Enkindle in me the fire of your Love.

Scripture: Psalm 51:4-6, 9, 11-14

Thoroughly wash away my guilt; and from my sin cleanse me.

For I know my transgressions; my sin is always before me.

Against you, you alone have I sinned; I have done what is evil in your eyes

So that you are just in your word, and without reproach in your judgment.

Cleanse me with hyssop, that I may be pure; wash me, and I will be whiter than snow.

Turn away your face from my sins; blot out all my iniquities.

A clean heart create for me, God; renew within me a steadfast spirit.

Do not drive me from before your face, nor take from me your Holy Spirit.

Restore to me the gladness of your salvation; uphold me with a willing spirit.

[Sit in silence for at least several minutes. If you struggle against distractions and nothing comes to you after a while, go about your day. Continue the below Questions for Reflection later on. Things may be revealed to you in events or interactions that take place throughout the day.]

Questions for Reflection

What are the most glaring faults that were revealed to me?

What part of these faults do I have an affection for? Do/did I secretly like or enjoy anything about these sins?

Try to imagine these faults, failings, or sins as the "friend" who is secretly an enemy. How has this enemy destroyed me? How has it robbed me of grace or caused damage to my life? St. Francis de Sales says, "Keep four things in mind: that by sin we have lost God's grace, lost our place in paradise, chosen the eternal flames of Hell, and rejected God's eternal love."

Describe the roots of these fault/failings. Are they jealousies, grudges, insecurities, wounds? What caused these weeds to grow in my heart?

What is one thing I can do today to begin to pull up these weeds? Perhaps I can pray for forgiveness, or say a kind word to someone I am jealous of, etc.?

Chapter Six: The Thorns

"In this Chamber of My Heart, the soul is more aware of the present moment. He understands the past must be committed to My Mercy - the future to My Provision. He opens himself up to the grace of the present moment."

~ Jesus to Maureen, January 26, 2001

In the first chamber, we address the weeds (our most glaring faults) that have been growing unchecked in the garden of grace. These are our most obvious sins. We start to recognize our dirtiness, and we make the resolution to clean ourselves up in the Living Water of the Holy Spirit. All this takes place in the "foyer" of Mary (the first chamber) and serves as a preparation of sorts so that we can enter the "House."

Now, what is the House? Simply put, it is the Heart of God.

From the first chamber, we move forward into the second chamber, which is the Heart of Jesus Christ. Now, I know this may be getting a little confusing, so let's look back at the map, the garden image. The second chamber is illustrated by a level of thorns. This is for a couple of reasons.

First, the classic image of the Sacred Heart of Jesus (as was revealed to St. Margaret Mary Alacoque) is surrounded by thorns. So this is a reminder of what we are doing when we enter this level. We are entering God.

Second, this stage is marked by the Crown of Thorns that Jesus wore in His Passion. What does His Crown of Thorns have to do with *your* spiritual journey? Allow me to explain.

If we look back on preceding chapters, you'll see that this journey follows the Passion of Jesus. In the first chapter, I discussed the "portal," going into the garden, into silence and prayer. This is similar to when Jesus entered the garden of Gethsemane. He entered silence and prayer. He was tempted viciously and had to surrender to the difficult journey ahead. This is like what souls experience when they first enter the garden, when they are tempted by the devil and have to themselves surrender to the spiritual journey ahead.

Then we discussed the "weeds" growing in the soul and the need for purification. (Theologians call this the Purgative stage.) Like I mentioned, here is where we recognize our most blatant sins. Here, we must begin to discipline our carnal desires and uproot sin. We must begin to tame the flesh. This is very much like our own, unique scourging -- though not nearly as brutal or gruesome as the Scourging that Jesus experienced in His Passion.

Now, we arrive at the Crowning with Thorns. (My Catholic friends will recognize that this is also following the Sorrowful Mysteries of the Rosary.) Here at the Crowning, we see Jesus bloodied from the scourging. They put on His head a crown made of long, sharp thorns and wrap Him in a purple cloak. They mock Him. They spit at Him. They hit Him. And He says nothing.

The all-powerful God of the universe (who could have struck them each down with a glance) says nothing. Instead of rising up and proving to them that He is a King, He allows them to mistreat Him. He accepts ridicule. He takes it. Why?

Because if He hadn't taken it, He wouldn't have died. If there hadn't been His death, there wouldn't have been His Resurrection. Or _ours_.

You see, the gates of Heaven were closed to human flesh after the sin of Adam and Eve. There needed to be a perfect atonement for that sin. And the only one who could offer _perfect_ atonement was God. The only way to reopen Heaven for the human family then was if God Himself approached the gates of Heaven in the form of human flesh... because God could not deny Himself. That would be like me denying myself entrance into my own house.

The point is, He accepted ridicule for _our_ sake. At the Crowning with Thorns, He thought not of Himself, but of us. Likewise, when we reach this next level of thorns, we no longer think of ourselves but of Him. We hear the voice of Pilate echoing in our hearts, _"Behold the Man!"_ (John 19:5) And things start to take a drastically different turn.

Up until this point in the journey, we've been looking at ourselves -- _our_ sins, what _we_ need to work on, where _we_ are going, the difficulties and temptations affecting _us_, etc. -- but now, the focus shifts. _"Behold the Man!"_

We actually behold the Son of God at the arrival of this second stage. We still need to work on purification, of course (because we are not yet perfected), but the spotlight moves from the journey to the one we journey for and with. In the second chamber, we encounter the living God, and we begin to _desire_ holiness. Like someone wandering in the desert who is given a few drops of cool water and can henceforth think of nothing but the spring. So we, when we encounter Him in this second chamber, begin to think primarily of _Him_.

Jesus told Maureen, "These souls thirst for holiness, thirst to please Me and draw closer to Me. To them this thirst seems unquenchable." (January 27, 2000)

It is kind of like becoming a parent. Before the child is born, you prepare. Moms begin "nesting." They begin cleaning the house and readying the room. Parents consider the cost. They discuss finances, employment, sometimes daycare. But once the child is born, the focus shifts.

Behold, the child.

The spotlight moves then onto their new son or daughter. They still continue cleaning the house, providing financially, and taking care of the necessary duties. But instead of doing these things because it's "what is supposed to be done," they now do these things because of _love_.

They are driven by the love of a real and tangible individual. Their thoughts are fixed on a person. They are mesmerized by the newness of the being. They are enchanted, enlivened. They begin to sacrifice for the sake of another, for the sake of love. This is how it is in the second chamber or the second level.

Jesus explained to Maureen, "...as the soul approaches the Second Chamber of My Heart, he begins his martyrdom of love; that is, he dies to his own free will as a sacrifice of love." (January 26, 2001)

In the second chamber, we not only enter the Heart of Jesus, we begin a relationship with Him.

As Jesus told Maureen, "The soul develops a private relationship with Me. Now the soul has light, but it is like a flame under cover, for much of the flame remains hidden between the soul and Me." (April 7, 2000)

Here we see Him, scourged, crowned, mocked... and we _feel_ for Him. From this point on, it's not just about getting rid of our faults. It's about getting rid of what hurts Him. We go from wanting to be on the journey to wanting to be with Him... wanting to please Him, console Him, love Him.

Here, it's like our hearts encounter His Heart, and the heat of its flame sets fire to us like a match. We are touched by Him, and we receive something from Him that changes us.

Jesus explained, "Here the soul receives much illumination, and interior changes take place within the heart." (April 7, 2000) Here, we receive our own thorns. The thorns that encircle the Sacred Heart of Jesus begin to wind around our hearts too. In this process, they actually pierce our hearts with a greater love for Him.

What's more, we are crowned upon our heads, just like He was crowned. This becomes the sign of our association with Him. The citizens of the Kingdom wear the King's crown. This is how He will recognize us. It's the symbol of our royalty in the Kingdom because it illustrates _what kind_ of a relationship we have with Him.

Allow me to explain.

This crown of thorns not only pierces our hearts with love for Him, but it also pierces our _minds_ too. It pierces us with keen awareness. St. Teresa of Avila says that, in the second mansion, "the understanding is keener and the faculties are more alert..." (pg 29)

In the second chamber, we receive an increased awareness of Him, as well as an awareness of the present moment -- the here and now. We begin to live in the "present" because that's where He lives.

The Blessed Mother told Maureen, "It is in the present moment that you will find God's presence most profoundly affecting your life and that of those around you..." (December 27, 1993)

The present moment is the defining moment. At the beginning of this book, I recalled the story of the disciples who Jesus condemned by saying, *"I never knew you. Depart from Me... "* (Matthew 7:23). I said that it was not enough to do deeds in His Name, but that we had to actually spend time with him in the garden. Remember that?

Now, I'm going to take that a step further and tell you it is not enough to just spend time with Him in the garden. We have to spend time with Him *in the present moment* in the garden.

I know. You might be getting confused. So, before I lose you, let me give you an example of what I mean.

Say there were a husband and wife who were just recently married. Every evening after work, they would come home to relax together. But the wife would sit in the living room, playing on her smartphone. Her husband would sit next to her, talk to her, tell her about his day, about his love for her. He would ask her questions about her day, but because of the distraction of her phone, she never heard him.

Occasionally she would nod as he talked, just to appease him, but she would never participate in the conversation. She was in the room with her husband, but not really "with" him. She was never aware of Him, never fully in the moment with him. Obviously, this couple is not going to advance in the marriage. They will not grow in intimacy. In fact, it will not take long until a relationship like this deteriorates completely.

Such is the case with our relationship with Jesus. Living in the present moment is a must. It is not enough to sit in the garden in silence with Him, distracted (like the wife who sits in the living room with her husband, distracted). It is not enough to rattle off an occasional, memorized prayer (like the wife who just nods, trying to appease her husband).

St. Francis de Sales stressed the importance of this in the second part of his *Introduction to the Devout Life*, "Retire at various times into the solitude of your own heart even while outwardly engaged in discussions or transactions with others. This mental solitude cannot be violated by the many people who surround you since they are not standing around your heart but only around your body. Your heart remains alone in the presence of God." (pg 86)

Friends, to pursue true holiness, we must be truly present with the Holy One. This means in every moment of the day. The crown we receive in the second chamber serves as a constant reminder to do this. It constantly probes an awareness of Him (both in our hearts and in our minds) while we are at work, at home, during recreation, in conversation, and in every trial that arises.

Jesus told Maureen, "... I desire only your well-being, never your detriment. Therefore, in every event of life, in every present moment, look for My Hand for I will bring good from all things." (May 25, 2001)

He later added, "...abandon yourselves completely to Me... This is the building block and the foundation of your holiness in every present moment. It is in this way I call you to perfection." (October 27, 2002)

Did you hear that? This is the way to _perfection_. The Blessed Mother confirmed this, too, saying, "...be sanctified, My dear children, always in the present moment, for here is your salvation." (July 29, 1995)

Some of you might be saying, _"the present moment... that's easy enough."_ But actually, it's quite difficult. Imagine the garden for a minute. Imagine three separate paths, side by side each other. They are very close to each other, almost touching. They all look nearly identical.

The middle path is the present moment. The path on the left is the past. The path on the right is the future. How easy it is, if we are not careful, to veer from the present and step into the past or future. What is the danger in that, you ask? Well, these paths don't all lead to the same destination.

The middle path, the present moment, leads to salvation, as the Blessed Mother said. The other two do not. The future and the past are paths that were carved out by the devil to lure you _away_ from salvation.

In her book _Interior Castle_, Saint Teresa said, "the devil wages a fierce war against us in the second mansions." (Page 28)

You see, Jesus lives in the present moment. God told Moses, "I am who am" (Exodus 3:14), which is _present_ tense. He did not say, "I am who _was_" or "I am who _will be_." He used the present tense to illustrate His eternal being in the never-ending present moment.

Therefore, the devil seeks to pull us from the present moment, and therefore from the presence of God and our eternal victory. It is only in the present moment that we experience God's Mercy and Provision, which are the keys to our success in this journey. When we live in the past, we reject His Mercy. We don't entrust the people or events of the past to His Mercy. We don't forgive ourselves or others, so we are stuck, so to speak, in the past, distanced from God, Who is in the present moment.

St. Peter told Maureen, "I wish to point out the two great temptations which most often rob the soul of the present moment. They are unforgiveness and guilt. Both of these temptations plunge the soul into the past. Both of these form great barriers between the human heart and the heart of God." (April 12, 2010)

Likewise, when we live in the future, we reject God's Provision. We don't entrust the events of the future to His Providence. We don't trust that He will provide and take care of us. So again, we are stuck, distanced from God on a separate path.

Friends, living in the present moment is absolutely crucial to arriving at the goal, to experiencing the victory. But, the crown of awareness does not end there. It makes us cognizant of still more. (Perhaps that's why theologians call this the Illuminative stage.) In addition to our awareness of Him and of the present moment, our minds are also pierced with knowledge of the Father's will for us.

We begin to see that our will isn't always what's best for us... after all, it's what led us into the dark outer area in the first place. So we begin to consider the Will of God. We consider His Ordaining Will, which authored and planned our life. And we consider His Permitting Will, which allows things to happen outside His original plan, which He uses for our greater good. In the second chamber, we begin to esteem God's Will. We begin to trust in it. Most importantly, we begin to surrender to it.

This is how to advance in the garden, from chamber to chamber. This is how we move deeper and deeper into the Heart of God: by surrendering more and more to His Will.

St. Teresa of Avila said, "All that the beginner... has to do -- and you must not forget this, for it is very important -- is to labor and be resolute and prepare himself with all possible diligence to bring his will into conformity with the will of God... This comprises the very greatest perfection, which can be attained on the spiritual road." (pg32)

I said earlier that, in this chamber, our hearts encounter His Heart and the heat of its flame sets fire to us like a match. We are a small match resting in God, resting in the furnace that enkindled it. What happens to a match like that? The fire consumes it, and bit by bit, the match is burned up. Little by little, our will diminishes, and God's will flourishes. God's will flourishes in us and, therefore, in the world too. In the words of St. John the Baptist, "He must increase. I must decrease." (John 3:30)

Here we begin the "melting away" of self. We begin to embrace the Divine Will and conform to the image and likeness of God. Jesus explained the importance of this to Maureen, "...every victory that is won is accomplished through your surrender to the Divine Will; for without Me, you can do nothing--with Me-- all things. The greatest measure of My grace comes to those who trust. It is trustful surrender that enables Me to draw souls into the deepest Chambers..." (September 19, 2002)

So much takes place within the soul in this second chamber that it is almost impossible to describe it all. We receive such an internal awareness in mind and heart that it probes dramatic change in us. Outwardly, though, people might not notice any change in us at all.

But everything _is_ different. It is as though the great mysteries of the spiritual life were veiled, and now the curtain is opened like a blind man who regains his sight. To outsiders, he may look the same as he did when he was sightless. But in actuality, his life has been completely transformed, simply because of his new awareness, because of the new way he perceives everything around him. Such is the case for the soul in the second chamber. This soul is transformed by his new awareness of God within.

What's more: after regaining his sight, the formerly blind man does not go back to sitting in his dark room. He goes out into the world -- exploring and sightseeing -- seeking to fully experience life. Likewise, the soul in the second chamber does not go back to his former ways. He goes deeper into the spiritual world -- through prayer and the sacraments -- seeking to fully experience the spiritual life.

The awareness gained in the second chamber causes the soul to turn to prayer, and the sacraments with greater fervor. Prayer and the sacraments then draw the soul deeper and deeper into the garden until the final destination of complete union is reached.

St. Francis de Sales spoke at length about the importance of prayer and the sacraments in the second part of his *Introduction to the Devout Life*. He says, "Since prayer places our intellect in the brilliance of God's light and exposes our will to the warmth of his Heavenly love, nothing else so effectively purifies our intellect of ignorance and our will of depraved affections."

So begin now. Allow the thorns of awareness to pierce your mind and heart. Let the fire of His Heart consume your will. Begin, right here, right now. There's no time like the present (moment).

Meditation

"My Will for you is to be, to *live* in the present moment. You have not grasped the power that is available to you there. I have called your mind to this for a reason... It is capable of going to deep places with me, but the devil uses my handiwork to ruin you. He uses your mind's great capacities and bombards it with clutter and busyness. He overloads it and hopes it will reach a shutdown. He hopes it will break your trust with fear and anxiety. He hopes that it will, at some point, reach such a state that it removes you completely from reality, from truth. I am truth. I am now... I Am who Am. See now, child, how important it is to keep a healthy mind. Here is truly the battlefield. For now, let go of everything that binds you -- and today, live with me." *(An excerpt from "Mornings with my Father" by Stacy Mal.)*

Prayer

Lord, Jesus, I am not worthy to enter under your roof, but only say the words, and my soul shall be healed. Allow me, here in this moment, to be crowned with your thorns. Pierce my mind with an increasing awareness of your presence in me and a new knowledge of who You are in truth. Pierce my heart with a greater love for You. Set fire to my soul, oh Lord. Lead me deeper into the spiritual garden until I find complete unity with your most Sacred Heart. Amen.

Scripture

"We also know that the Son of God has come and has given us discernment to know the one who is true. And we are in the one who is true, in His Son Jesus Christ. He is the true God and eternal life." (1 John 5:20)

Questions for Reflection

Enter into the present moment, and "Behold the Man!" Picture Jesus' face. Picture where He is. Picture yourself with Him. What is He doing? What is He saying to you?

God calls us to put aside our will and surrender to His Will in all things. Is there currently an area of life where you feel God is calling you to deeper surrender and trust? Are you finding it difficult to put aside your will regarding a particular practice, desire, or belief?

Have you ever met someone with blind faith and witnessed their complete surrender? If so, what was most impactful about the way they lived their faith?

What is one practical thing I can do from here on out to remind myself of the present moment throughout the day?

Chapter Seven: Direction and Blooms

"My child, I wish to cultivate in the garden of your soul the virtue of Holy Love. This virtue made it possible for the first Apostles to spread the Faith to foreign lands. It is through Holy Love the soul chooses to love God with the whole heart and neighbor as self. Holy Love enables you to look past obvious flaws of character in those you meet and see a soul journeying on the path of salvation much as your own. It is Holy Love that turns the soul away from the world and self and towards My Son."

~ Blessed Mother to Maureen, August 27, 1993

Before we get into the third chamber (the blooms), I want to first talk about direction. When you look at a regular map, it almost always has direction arrows on it, right? North, South, East, and West. Well, this garden map is no different. If you want to get to the center of the Garden -- to the depths of God, to the heights of Heaven -- you need to be going in the right direction.

What would happen if I gave you directions to a theatre in your city, and I just told you to take Main Street all the way there, but I didn't tell you whether to go North or South on Main Street? Does it matter? Of course, it matters! It matters a lot! It's not enough to just take Main Street. You have to be going in the right direction on Main Street towards your goal. The same is true in the garden.

If you look at the direction arrows on your map of the garden, you will see that it just says HL and SL. If we start at the gate of Mary, we want to go HL (North) toward the Tree of Life. Right?

If we go in any other direction -- if we go SL (East or West) even slightly -- then what happens? We will miss the goal. Eventually, we will end up back outside the gate, in the outer area, right?

OK, so, what is HL and SL??

Well, HL stands for Holy Love. Holy Love is the foundation of all the messages Heaven has given to Maureen Sweeney Kyle (hence the name, Holy Love Ministries). If God's love is called Divine Love, then human love is called Holy Love. We seek holiness by loving.

Basically, Holy Love is the two great commandments: "To love God above all else and your neighbor as yourself," which is found in Matthew 22:36-40. There, Jesus said, "All the Law and the Prophets hang on these two commandments."

So, you see, this is the direction. If we live these two commandments at every moment, we continually take steps North in the garden. Sometimes we may take small steps in Holy Love, and sometimes we may take big steps. Either way, when we walk in Holy Love (when we love God above all else and neighbor as self), we continually move deeper into God, toward the ultimate goal, which is union with God.

Here's the thing: as we begin to live in Holy Love, we move closer to the source of Love and become bearers of it. Think of it this way. We _show_ love, but God _is_ Love. It is like God is the sun (a being of intense heat, light, and fire), and we are windows that allow others to experience that heat, light, and warmth. Try as we might, we could never become the sun. We merely become clean enough to reveal the sun.

Or if I could use the match example from the last chapter. God is like the sun, and we are a match. We have no light or heat or flame of our own, but if we move close enough to the sun, we can be lit by Him and thereby affect others with the flame He gives us. We can even move so close to Him that we are _in_ Him, that our little match is fully consumed by Him. This is what St. Paul means when he said, "It is no longer I who live but He who lives in me." (Galatians 2:20)

The direction of Holy Love is crucial. St. Teresa of Avila said, "Let us realize... that true perfection consists in the love of God and of our neighbor, and the more nearly perfect is our observance of these two commandments, the nearer to perfection we shall be."

Understand, too, that if Divine Love is God's Love and Holy Love is human love, then the Blessed Mother is the epitome of Holy Love. This is because she was sinless --the only sinless human (besides Jesus, who is God) to ever exist. She exemplified Holy Love. She loved God above all else and Her neighbor as herself in a most perfect way.

So, the Immaculate Heart of Mary _is_ Holy Love, just in the same way that the Sacred Heart of Jesus _is_ Divine Love. The grace that Mary gives us, then, always nurtures Holy Love in us. This is another reason why the Immaculate Heart of Mary (the epitome of Holy Love) is inscribed on the gateposts. Holy Love is the summation of the Ten Commandments, the boundary lines for the garden of grace.

Now, that being said, what is SL? SL is self-love. Self-love is not about God or others. It's about me, me, me. I'll do this because it benefits me. I'll say that because it makes me look good. I'll avoid them because they rub me the wrong way. I don't believe in that moral truth because it offends me, and so forth and so on. Self-love is the opposite of Holy Love. And it always, in every circumstance, even if it seems slight, leads away from God. Always.

Now, this includes disordered love. Disordered love might not outwardly, on the surface, appear to be about "self." It might have another person as the supposed focal point. But if we place this other person above the love of God, then it is disordered love. It is out of order. Holy Love is to love God above all else (God first), and THEN we love neighbor as self. To love neighbor above all else, including and most especially above God and his laws, is disordered.

For example, say someone we love is committing mortal sin, and we choose to believe they should be allowed to commit that sin. In fact, say we go so far as to <u>want</u> them to be able to commit it because it makes them happy. We even go so far as to re-label it so that it's not mortal sin anymore. We call it a "right" that they should be allowed to enjoy.

This is disordered love. It has, at the very root of it, self-love. It is actually self-love in a pretty hat. Because here's the thing: if you have disordered love like this, it's because of one of two reasons. One, either you truly believe your way of thinking trumps God's way -- which is self-love because you love your ways over God's ways. Or, you really do believe it's God's law, but you don't want the persecution that might come as a result of living in the truth. That it is a mortal sin. This is also self-love because you love your reputation more than God's law -- actually, even more than your friend.

I know, I know. It's really hard to hear what I'm saying. This is not an easy pill to swallow. But listen, if you're in the garden,

Satan is going to tempt you in different ways, then he would tempt those in the outer court. Those in the outer court are already in his clutches. He just has to keep them busy, away from silence -- so they can neither see nor hear the call to enter. He just has to keep them in mortal sin and keep the passions of the flesh strong so that they can't control the reigns of their own horse, so to speak.

But you... you're already in the garden. You're already working on holiness. You've been instructed in mortal sin, confessed it, and are diligently trying to avoid it. So those kinds of temptations aren't going to work as well on you. He has to tempt you under the appearance of good.

Think about the way Satan tempted the first man and the first woman in the first garden. It was under the appearance of good. "The woman saw that the tree was _good_ for food and pleasing to the eyes, and the tree was desirable for gaining wisdom. So she took some of its fruit and ate it; and she also gave some to her husband, who was with her, and he ate it." (Genesis 3:6)

If you are a Christian, seriously working on Holy Love, then Satan will tempt you with something that seems good. He will tempt you with disordered or self-love -- false love -- in order to get you to head in another direction. Even if you veer ever so slightly, it's a turn away from the goal. Friends, if the devil has any virtue at all, it is patience (though we know it is false virtue because it is not done with love).

The devil is content if you make only a slight turn away from HL because He knows it's a start. You have moved away from the source of Light and will be easier to coerce from there on out. So he will start slow and then increase his temptations and attacks. He will wait you out. He knows eventually, those baby steps in SL will cause you to miss the mark.

St. Teresa of Avila said, "The devil sets about undermining the soul in trivial ways and involving it in practices which he makes the soul think are not wrong. Little by little, he darkens its understanding, and weakens its will, and causes SELF LOVE to increase, until... he begins to withdraw the soul from the love of God and persuades it to indulge in its own desires."

So you see, there are really only two kinds of **true** Love -- Divine Love and Holy Love. The goal of life is for these two "loves" to come together, to merge and unite as one for all eternity. St Teresa of Avila called this the "spiritual marriage." St. Francis de Sales called it the "excellence of the soul."

As we move through life (through the garden), we need to be constantly mindful -- in every moment, every situation, every relationship, every choice -- of the direction we are headed. We need to constantly ask ourselves: is this loving God above all else and neighbor as myself? If it's not, it's the wrong decision. Plain and simple.

OK, now, let's move on to level three. Looking at the map, you can see that level three starts with a flat green area and then basically turns into flowers and butterflies.

Friends, here is where we work on virtue. Here is where we are tried and tested. It's the fourth Sorrowful Mystery, where we carry our Cross. Here is where our steadfastness in prayer begins to bear fruit and become visible to others -- in the form of virtue. We now begin to _show_ patience, love, temperance, fortitude, etc. Level two was progress made in private with Jesus. Level three is where our faith blossoms for others to see.

But... before we go any further, I need to backtrack for a minute. I need to touch on something very important in the pursuit of virtue. I need to talk about the flesh. I would like to talk about physical health for just a minute. Now, you might be thinking, "*what does that have to do with the spiritual journey*?" Well, it has everything to do with it.

Bear with me.

Here's a scenario for you: Say my daughter gets accepted to a college 15 hours away, and I want to buy her a car so that she can get home from school. Would I buy her a lemon? No! Would I be concerned if she got in an accident and then tried to drive that banged-up car home? Yes! Why? Because that's the vehicle that keeps her safe and gets her back home to me. It has to be in good shape.

Now, what does physical health have to do with the spiritual journey? Friends, your body is your vehicle to get you back home to the Father. God is concerned about your body (your temple) the same way I would be concerned about my daughter's car. But infinitely more so. As much as we journey in the deep -- in prayer and in the garden -- we journey also in the body. We cannot escape this fact.

But here's the thing: the devil -- who knows how important the vehicle is -- has been working VERY hard in recent years to break down the body. He's been patiently coercing those in charge of our food supply, getting them to add chemicals to it that, at best, damage the body, create disease, cause food addiction, inflammation, and other things. In fact, these chemicals slowly poison us to death. Modern medicine then creates another drug, another chemical, to try and take away the adverse effects instead of trying to rebuild and reverse the damage.

Maybe you're reading this thinking I've lost it, that this isn't the time or place to be talking about this. Maybe you're thinking I've flipped, that I don't know what I'm talking about. But, friends, I _do_ know what I'm talking about. I used to weigh about 280 pounds. (Actually, I stopped weighing myself at 280. I could have been quite a bit more than that.) I've also had numerous heart procedures. I used to take about twenty prescription pills a day in my early-to-mid 20s. I've struggled with anxiety and depression, blood sugar imbalances, pain, cysts, digestive issues, hormone problems, Dysautonomia, you name it. And much of this started when I was a child.

Today, though, I rarely struggle with any of these issues. So, did I experience some miraculous healing? Yes, I did. But not in the way you think, not in the way that I prayed for.

I used to cry out to God for healing, daily, for years. I used to beg Him, "Just take it away! Lay Your Hand on me and let it be gone."

But He did not do that. He chose to heal me in another completely different way -- education. He chose to teach me about my body, about our food supply, about natural health, and the power of phytonutrients and herbals -- and slowly, I began to take back my health. I began to rebuild my temple. It was not just for my benefit, though. It was for yours as well.

If God wanted to heal me just for my sake, He would have probably done it the way I asked -- quickly, miraculously, without explanation or reason. But He chose to teach me, over the course of many years, because He knew I would not keep this information to myself. He knew I would share it with you and anyone who I'd encounter.

What does this have to do with the garden? Why am I bringing this up now, before I talk about the third chamber, which is the virtues? Because no matter how hard I tried back then, I could not be virtuous or holy. I could not find the joy of the Lord in depression. I could not trust Him in anxiety. I could not serve Him in pain. I could not pray in fatigue. I could not practice patience with raging hormones. I could not practice temperance with erratic blood sugars and chemical-induced food addiction.

Back then, it was failure after failure after failure. Life got harder. Depression got worse. And ironically, I got further and further away from where I wanted to be, spiritually.

I didn't put it all together, though, until I had a monumental and life-changing conversation with my spiritual director. I was crushed by my numerous failures, and he looked at me and said, "You are trying to become holy."

I nodded, "Yes."

He then said, very slowly, "Holy is healthy, and healthy is holy."

Let me repeat that for you. "Holy is healthy, and healthy is holy."

I prayed about those words for weeks. I had to take a step back and look at myself as a _whole_ person. Up until that time, I had my physical life completely separate from my spiritual life. There was a disconnect within me, and I couldn't figure out why I was such a mess.

I hated myself for not being able to fast during Lent, for being a terrible glutton. But, you know, when you're blood sugars are at 38, you just want to eat, and you eat ravenously... regardless if it's Ash Wednesday or Good Friday. Blood sugars don't care about the calendar.

Now, please, I am not - NOT - saying that if you're not healthy, you're not holy. And neither was my spiritual director. There are chosen souls who God allows to experience disease as _part_ of their journey and their call to holiness. Some, actually, are like gold tested in the fire of disease. I will talk to you about one such soul, my friend Patti, in the next chapter.

But some of us, though, have been chosen for health, called to life, and are simply being sabotaged. The devil is convincing us to put peanut butter in our gas tank and then watching us cry when we can't move forward.

Friends, a good portion of the ingredients in packaged processed foods, should not be put in the human body. God didn't make these things. He didn't make our bodies with the ability to digest them. Sometimes, even seemingly-natural foods are so processed and changed that the body barely recognizes them as food anymore.

Many of these have a real negative effect on the body. They cause the body to react in severe ways. And these reactions can be so inhibiting to the development of virtue that they act like Round-Up in the spiritual garden.

Healthy is holy, and holy is healthy. What my spiritual director was saying that day is that there is holiness in taking your health seriously and looking at the body from God's perspective, as a temple. As St. Paul said, _"Do you not know that your body is a_ *temple of the Holy Spirit within you, whom you have from God, and that you are not your own? For you have been purchased at a price. Therefore, glorify God in your body."* (1 Corinthians 6:19-20)

When I started looking at my body (my physical flesh) as a temple, that was life-changing for me. It's even the name of my ministry now: Rebuilding Your Temple. For a while, I was just focused on the spiritual aspect, writing and giving retreats...but I have since received my certification as a health coach, and I have become a distributor of natural, plant-based supplements too. I have merged the physical and spiritual to help people rebuild the whole temple.

I know I got a little off-topic there, but my point is: God cares about your health. If He didn't care about the body, Jesus wouldn't have healed it so many times when He walked the earth! So please, begin to look at the whole person. Begin to consider what you put into your body. Begin to consider whether your flesh is helping you in the journey or hurting you.

If you are drinking many cans of soda a day, getting drunk several times a week, or eating a ton of sugar on a daily basis; if your diet is full of processed, canned, and boxed food, or if you drink so much caffeine you cannot sleep... understand there's truth in the old adage, "garbage in, garbage out." You're going to feel terrible, and you are going to have a hard time on this journey -- especially in the third chamber.

So I encourage you (I beg you) to take this seriously, to read food labels and try and buy more natural options. If you need help with this, please ask me. Contact me via my website at www.StacyMal.com. This is so near and dear to my heart.

OK, now back to the third level, the buds, and blooms of virtue. Here is where the hard work you've done in secret -- the pruning and weeding -- becomes visible to others in the form of virtue. Like a butterfly that leaves the private life of the cocoon, here's where we see what you're made of. Here's where we see your true colors. Here's where you learn to fly.

The bible says, "by their fruits, you will know them." (Matthew 7:20) Some virtuous people have beautiful, sweet blooms. But there are other people who do not. The outer layers of their buds _seem_ normal, but when it unfolds to reveal its inner self, there is only darkness. For some people, they've been drinking polluted water and growing polluted blooms. And when push comes to shove, we see that. By the natural progression of the journey, we each uncover our true selves eventually.

This is why this journey is so important. Your garden begins to beautify the world we live in. Here's where the true foliage of your patience, kindness, and compassion becomes medicine for the people in your life and in the world around you.

And friends, those people are very important. God gives each of us opportunities to practice virtue over and over -- in our vocation! Our vocation is the unique path that God himself carved out for us. For some, it is the path of parenthood; for some, it is the single life, and for others, it is the religious life. Whatever the vocation is, that is the path that contains the most grace for you. Which means it is the path capable of producing the most buds. It's the straightest, most-assured path YOU can take to the Tree of Life, to the Heart of God.

It is important to understand that while we live in this earthly dimension, most of us don't stay in prayer and silence all day long. Like in our house, the garden is a place of rest. A place where we relax and experience love. It is a place where we gather strength before going outside to work and serve.

Such is the case here too. The garden is your true home. You carry it with you always, never really separated from it, never "homeless," never wanting or lacking. But, we must leave silence and devotion in order to put into practice all that we are being taught there. We must do the duties required of us by our vocation. Like the student who leaves the classroom to enter the field, so we must leave devotion to enter our vocation. Our spirituality should not consist of only the garden. The garden is the foundation, not the entirety.

And please, don't think you're totally in the clear here. Stage three also requires a great deal of reflection, hard work, and self-knowledge.

St. Teresa of Avila said, " If you think you have all virtue, you do not." .... She says, "the devil will run a thousand times around hell if by doing so he can make us believe that we have a single virtue which we have not." Continually pray for humility then, and self-awareness.

One other thing to keep in mind: it's not uncommon at this stage, as we emerge from the weeds and thorns, to find that we have a tick or two attached to us. Sometimes we find even a garden snake has slithered into our boot or latched onto our shirt. These friends are attachments that took hold of us in the outer court or early in the journey. Sometimes we are attached to a relationship, a possession, a goal, our image, our social status, our money, etc. These things need to be purged now too.

These are not sins or faults, or bad habits. They are simply things very close to us that we hang onto. Things that nip at us infect us and weaken us for the journey. They are things that have become, over time, like a false security blanket. Maybe we are codependent in a relationship or bound to the perception of others.

Whatever the attachment is, these affect the way we think, the way we act, and the decisions we make...and not for good. They compete with our goal. They often distort the direction and prohibit steps in Holy Love. Like a chain that ties us to the outer court or the inner levels, we reach a point where we can only go so far as long as we still have these. We can't move forward anymore until we are stripped of them and freed of them.

Some of you, up until now, haven't wanted to be free of these. So I have to ask you: which do you prefer... the chain or the celestial paradise? Which do you prefer, bondage or freedom?

Meditation

"The garden is blooming, child. So many things that you did not see or notice before will begin to take form. They will begin to come forth, to bloom. Let us marvel together at the newness, the beauty. Let Me teach you of each new bud. Let me explain its purpose as it unfolds. Let my light shine upon it. Let My Breath tickle it to motion. I do not need you to do anything at this point. Just watch... as the secret place of our meeting (the garden of your heart) experiences springtime. Just watch. See all that your Father has planted. See how I have been caring for you from the beginning. Soon we shall see the fruit of My handiwork in you. Soon the seeds that I planted long ago -- the plants that I have had to prune along the way -- will produce a plentiful harvest for starving souls. I am doing this, not you. You shall see. Just continue to come to Me here in the stillness. Let Me point out the growth, the new life, the new blooms. Do not get so busy that you do not come to Me or that you overlook some new growth... as each one is important for your understanding. Child, I have not randomly planted. I did not scatter seed carelessly or aimlessly upon the soil of your heart. No, I plotted a meticulously designed garden, one seed at a time, each to bloom at a very specific time and place. Slow down and look. Do not hurry or rush My design. Much of its glory comes from the anticipation of the bud. Be patient. Sit with me. You have much to learn regarding these signs of life. I Myself will teach you. Receive my peace, child.... *(An excerpt from "Mornings with my Father" by Stacy Mal.)*

Prayer

Lord, Jesus, you have created me and molded me in the secret recesses of your Divine Will, like that of a cocoon. I ask You now for the strength and the grace to advance still further. Give me wings, Lord, that I may ascend new heights in the spiritual life. Help me fly upwards toward your majesty through the practice of virtue. Heal me of all Self Love. Uphold me in Holy Love. Grant me new life in You. Amen.

Scripture

"Just so, every good tree bears good fruit, and a rotten tree bears bad fruit. A good tree cannot bear bad fruit, nor can a rotten tree bear good fruit. Every tree that does not bear good fruit will be cut down and thrown into the fire. So by their fruits, you will know them." (Matthew 7:17-20)

Questions for Reflection

Do you ever feel the pull in a different direction than HL (Holy Love)? At what times is it most difficult to resist SL (Self-Love) or DL (Disordered Love)?

Is there someone in your life who always seems to be moving in the direction of HL? What types of things do they do/say that lead you to believe this?

The Catechism says there are Three Theological Virtues: faith, hope, and love. In your opinion, which is the most important?

Catechism says there are Four Cardinal Virtues: prudence, justice, fortitude, and temperance. In your opinion, which is the most difficult?

"Health is holy, and holy is healthy." What are some common health issues today that might make it more difficult to work towards holiness and the practice of virtue?

St. Teresa of Avila, "Even those who advance through the chambers are not entirely secure. The devil attacks under the guise of doing good.... he sets about undermining the soul in trivial ways and involving it in practices which he makes the soul think are not wrong. Little by little, he darkens its understanding, and weakens its will, and causes SELF LOVE to increase, until... he begins to withdraw the soul from the love of God and persuades it to indulge in its own desires."

Have you ever felt the Devil tempt you in the way St. Teresa describes it?

Chapter Eight: The Embrace & the Tree

"Child, in the acceptance of every cross, is the victory of Satan's defeat. The cross is the light on the path of Holy Love. The more you embrace the cross, which is God's Will, the deeper you are plunged in My Heart to be nourished and guarded. No cross comes to you against God's Will."

~ Blessed Mother to Maureen, September 14, 1994

So far, we've been talking about the journey to the center of the garden. Our main goal is union with God. St. Teresa called this the *Spiritual Marriage*. St. Francis De Sales called it the *Excellence of the Soul*. But it's the same thing. It's union with God. It is essentially the big, red X on the map. It's actually a big, red heart if you think about it. But it's where we are headed -- the depths of the Sacred Heart of Jesus, united with the Heart of the Eternal Father, living in unity with the Holy Spirit.

In John 17:21-23, Jesus prays, *"as you, Father, are in me and I in you, [may] they also may be in us..."*

This is the goal. We're being drawn and led through each level, each chamber, in order to accomplish this. Think of it this way: an adult child is traveling home to see his father. After much traveling, he enters his hometown, then his old neighborhood, then the street he grew up on, which takes him to his father's house. He drives onto the property. He parks the car and actually enters his father's house. He sees his father. Then, finally, they embrace.

You feel the build in the son's journey as he gets nearer and nearer to His father. Such is the case with this garden journey also. In each level or chamber, there is more build, more excitement as we get closer and closer to our Heavenly Father. The fulfillment of the garden journey is the full, complete, and eternal _embrace_ of God the Father.

It's important to remember the big picture as we move through the garden. It's important not to lose sight of how exciting each level is. Each small victory at any level is a big victory in the garden because it brings you that much closer to your eternal reward.

Try to envision this journey as if you were watching it from Heaven, from God's eyes. Sometimes we get so caught up in the difficulties -- the pruning, the weeding, the detachment -- that we forget where this is all leading. Our goal in this journey is union with God. It is the eternal embrace of the Most Holy Trinity -- the God of pure Love, full Light, and complete Peace. Everything in this world is building, culminating, leading towards that (or in some cases, moving away from it).

Unlike a regular journey, though -- where you know it's exactly 25 miles, or you know it takes approximately 10 hours -- there is no "timetable" for this spiritual journey through the garden. You could spend 20 years in the first level and two days in the second level. Or vice versa.

2 Peter 3:8 says, _"with the Lord, one day is like a thousand years and a thousand years like one day."_

What determines how long the journey takes is our surrender, putting aside _our_ will, and accepting _God's_ Will. In order to embrace the Father, we must first embrace His Will.

This journey is not the succession of miles or minutes like a typical journey, but rather a series of "yeses" to God's Will. I believe this is true because God transcends time and space. He is not bound by it and does not operate in it. His minute markers, therefore, are not minutes at all but rather "fiats."

You see, we look at the clock and say, "I'm going to do this at 11:30, and I'm going to do that at 12:00."

But God says, *"I'm going to do this when she says yes, and I'm going to do that when he says yes."*

It does not matter if it takes one day or a thousand years to hear that, yes. God's "time" (His plan) moves forward with the "yes." And each yes is like a domino that sets the next one in motion.

In fact, the human yes is so very important that I believe the world itself would still be waiting for a savior if Our Lady had not said yes at the Annunciation. There was no plan B for that moment. There is no plan B for the moment you are in now.

In fact, you could say that the plan of God, His very "clock," stands still as He waits for your yes. Friends, just like you, cannot arrive at noon without first experiencing 11:30 and 11:50. So, too, you cannot experience the great blessing God has in store for you without first giving Him the minute markers -- the "yeses." It is the "yes" that moves His hand forward, the "yes" that enables the journey to progress onward.

I cannot tell you how many times this has happened to me, where I was praying for something that just wasn't happening, and God was waiting on me to surrender it to Him. Years ago, I was praying about our finances. We had so much medical debt from my health issues and our kids' health issues. I was only working part-time and looking for extra work, looking for ways to climb out of this gigantic pit. We had to sell our house and move into a rental. It was terrible.

I just kept praying for God to provide. But nothing was happening. In fact, every time I went to pray, it was like he was ignoring me because he never really spoke to me about our debt. Instead, God began urging me to have another baby.

I remember being in prayer like, *"uh, yeah, but.. that's not what I had in mind."*

I had gone through a series of health issues, we were still going through the kids' health issues, and my pregnancies were rough -- so rough. I always ended up on bed rest, always in the hospital, and the postpartum depression that followed was always a nightmare. Besides, I knew I needed to work. We needed money. Bad. How could we afford another baby? If I worked, I would have to put the baby in daycare, which I didn't want to do... and that would cost money also.

When God spoke this to my heart, my heart fought it, BIGTIME. I argued with God and continued to pray for finances. And _nothing_ happened. (Side note: don't argue with God. You never win.)

Finally, God's urging was so strong I actually began to _grieve_ the baby I was not choosing. I did. In a very real and intense way, I began to suffer the "loss" of that baby before it was even conceived. It sounds insane, I know. But it happened. And it was awful.

I believe what happened was that God shared a piece of His Heart with me. He let me feel a small fraction of what He felt as a result of our decision not to conceive. Because, in truth, that baby was already very much "alive" in the mind and heart and will of God, even if I had not consented to conception. The heartache that I felt -- and God felt --was awful.

A long story short, my husband and I agreed to have another baby. We were pregnant almost immediately after the decision. The pregnancy was very rough, just like I expected. And, as it turned out, I was carrying twins. I miscarried one of them, and then I almost died in labor.

But my nurse that day was named Mary, and I gave birth to a beautiful baby girl named Abby. Her name actually means, "My Father in rejoicing." (Though we did not discover this until much later after she was born and after we had named her.) I did get postpartum depression afterward. In fact, it was the worst case of it out of all of my pregnancies. And it was everything I feared, really, if I am honest.

However, doors opened up wide after her birth. I was hired full time a few weeks after she was born and began working _from home_ with the babysitting next to me. We suddenly found extra "side jobs" in addition to that too. And in less than one year's time, we paid off all our medical debt and even saved enough money to buy a new house. And the most beautiful thing was that our family was better off for having this new baby. Oh my goodness, she brought so much joy and light to our home... to every single person living in our house. We were changed forever, in ways I couldn't have dreamed.

You see, I was praying for _my_ will, but God was waiting for me to surrender to _His_ will. He was waiting for me to trust Him. I believe we would still be renting and drowning financially if we would not have said yes to that baby. We said yes to life, and God gave us life beyond measure, not just with the baby, but in all other areas too. He even gave us a fourth baby a few years later.

Now, this is hard, I know. To surrender our will, to surrender what we want with our life -- where we want to go, what we want to become, how we see it all play out. These things are often what drive us in life. But, over time, they become like an internal compass too. They become the thing we consult first. But, friends, listen: that compass is broken, it's flawed. You can't trust it. If you want to get to that fourth level, which is the center of the garden, you need to throw away that compos.

You might say, *"if I get rid of my compass, how will I know where I'm going? Won't that be walking blindly through life?"* Yes. Yes, it will be. And that's the whole point. You don't need a compass. You have a real, live guide leading you -- a guide who foresees every single thing up ahead. Walking blindfolded strengthens your trust. Your trust produces your yes and perfects your surrender.

In the case of the garden, the "yes" opens up new doorways and new passageways into new levels. If you can perfect the yes -- if you can perfect your surrender to His will -- you can arrive at level four, which is conformity with God's will. It is the embrace of God. It's union. Friends, it's Heaven.

A message Jesus gave to Maureen sums it up, ”The souls, and few there are, whom I select from the third chamber as My saints and martyrs of love come into the fourth and most intimate chamber. They have been perfected in Holy Love. They have purged themselves of the smallest fault or attachment, which has been an obstacle between their heart and Mine. They have successfully defeated Satan in his discouragements. These are the souls that are able to accept all things as from the Hand of God -- that is, God's Will for them. These souls always trust in Divine Providence. The virtues have been honed and fine-tuned in their lives. They no longer live for themselves, but I live through them."

St. Paul puts it this way in Galatians 2:20, *"My old self has been crucified with Christ. It is no longer I who live, but Christ who lives in me."*

Crucified with Christ. Please understand: this journey we are called to is the way of the Cross. As I said before, this follows the Sorrowful Mysteries of the Rosary. Actually, the garden journey follows <u>all</u> the Mysteries of the Rosary. (For more information, look for the *Garden Rosary Prayer Book* by Stacy Mal to come soon.)

Think about it. Jesus started His passion by going into prayer IN A GARDEN, the garden of Gethsemane. We have no other way to the Father except through Him, with Him, in Him. So, we too, start in the garden. We, too, then begin our passion. We begin the ascent to Calvary, up the mountain of the Lord, deep within us.

We are scourged by pruning, stripped in detachment, and we fall down in tests of virtue. We surrender to God's will and put our will to death. We die to ourselves and rise to new life. Everything culminates toward this -- the Cross. Friends, the wood of the Cross that He hung upon on Calvary, is the new Tree of Life. It's the tree that illuminates the garden, the tree from which the Living Water of God flows.

When we die to ourselves, we nail our passions and our will to the Cross of Christ. We are thereby grafted onto the Tree of Life. We become one with Him. At the top of that mountain, we are _transfigured_ by His eternal Light (like He was transfigured on Mt. Tabor in Luke 9:28-36).

And I know, looking at the garden and all the hard work that we have to accomplish beforehand might make the goal seem far off, even discouraging. But, I'm going to share a secret with you. You can experience this also by receiving the Eucharist.

As Catholics, we believe that Jesus is truly present -- Body, Blood, Soul, and Divinity -- in the Eucharist. We believe that we take His true presence into ourselves. Now, think about that for a minute. Really, think about it.

Normally, when speaking of food, the lesser assimilates into the greater. The food particle breaks down and becomes part of the body. Bread is digested and becomes part of us. It nourishes, builds up, and strengthens the body, right?

Well, here's the thing: when it comes to the Eucharist, we are the lesser, and He is the greater. The ingredients of the host might be digested by our bodies, but through the Eucharist, WE are actually incorporated into HIM. Therefore, the more often we receive the Eucharist, the more like Him we become. Like one who continually exposes himself to the sun, and becomes then colored by its rays, so we become like the Son of God when we expose our inner souls to His glory.

Think about this. The goal of this journey -- union with God -- is available to us via a small piece of bread. I think a lot of times, we are desensitized to the awesomeness and mystery of the

Eucharist. We don't reflect often enough on the fact that the Sacred Heart at the center of the garden is available to us daily.

Protestants -- even many Catholics -- have deduced the Eucharist to a mere symbol. If you are one of these people, then I have to ask you: if you find it difficult to believe that God can clothe Himself in bread and wine, do you also find it difficult to believe in the Incarnation?

Because here's the thing: God is not flesh. He _became_ flesh. God is Spirit and Love. But He put on flesh and became Man to be with us. Why, then, can't He become bread and wine to be _in_ us? If everything culminates towards this unity between God and man, then it only makes sense God would take the Incarnation a step further. It only makes sense that He would draw us closer and closer. First, He came in the flesh to be _with_ us; then He came in bread to be _in_ us.

Friends, listen. This inner area of the garden -- the peak of the mountain -- is the promised land. And every communion you receive is a foretaste of it. Think for a minute of the story of the Israelites' journey out of Egypt, found in the book of Exodus. It foreshadows this very journey.

- The Israelites were held captive in Egypt, as slaves, in bondage. Just like we are in the dark area, the outer court.
- Then, they are called out of this bondage by Moses. We are called out -- or rather, called _in_ --by the Blessed Virgin Mary.
- The Israelites begin the journey. They cross the red sea into safety. We cross the garden gate via Confession, into a state of grace, which is safety.

- They then receive their direction, the Ten Commandments. The direction in the garden is Holy Love, the summation of the Ten Commandments.

- The Israelites begin to grumble along the journey. They feel like they are starving because in Egypt, they fed the flesh with rich, luscious food, and now in the desert they are doing without. In the first chamber of the garden, we also must tame the desires of the flesh (and we sometimes grumble in the process).

- The Israelites then build the tabernacle, according to God's exact design. In the second chamber, we, too, become aware of God's plan and begin building a tabernacle in our hearts through prayer and the sacraments.

- Then God comes to dwell in the tabernacle of the Israelites. He makes Himself visible -- like a cloud by day and a pillar of fire at night. In the third chamber of the garden, the living water of God waters the garden into full bloom. God makes Himself visible in us through the virtues we display.

- Finally, the Israelites take possession of the promised land. And so do we. We are united with God -- we take possession of Him -- and inherit the promised Kingdom of Heaven.

The Lord tells the Israelites in Joshua 1:7, *"Only be strong and steadfast, being careful to observe the entire law which Moses my servant enjoined on you. Do not swerve from it either to the right or to the left, that you may succeed wherever you go."* He tells them not to swerve from the law -- the summation of which is Holy Love, HL. Do not go to the left or right... do not go into Self Love, SL.

The Israelites went through many, MANY battles before reaching the promised land. We also do in the pursuit of salvation. We fight against ourselves and our carnal desires. We fight against the devil and his legion of demons, who never cease tempting us. It should bring us hope then, that in chapter 21, verse 43-44, the Israelites succeed. " *The LORD gave Israel the entire land he had sworn to their ancestors he would give them. Once they had taken possession of it and dwelt in it, the LORD gave them* _peace_ *on every side, just as he had promised their ancestors."*

Peace on every side. Peace. I know, even when looking at this journey from the standpoint of the Israelites, the Victory can sometimes seem hard to relate to. What is this peace? What does sainthood really look like today?

Well, I was privileged enough to witness the journey of one such soul who I believe in my heart achieved this victory.

Her name is Patti Kirschner. She was a wife and mother of five and a very DEAR friend of mine. Several years ago, Patti and I were in a small rosary prayer group together. We did the St. Louis de Montfort 33-day consecration to Jesus through Mary. And shortly after this consecration, Patti found out she had breast cancer. When we talked about it, we wondered about the timing. I can still see her sitting there saying, "It's ironic that this is right after our consecration, isn't it?" Looking back, I see it was divine. Her journey started with Mary, and she was heading toward Jesus. Sound familiar?

As she prayed about her situation, she said she heard the word "Victory" in her heart. She believed this meant she would overcome cancer, and it seemed to give her hope and strength.

The treatment option she chose involved extensive time in California - which is quite far from Pennsylvania and her family.

It was hard for her, being so far away. But while in California, she entered the garden in a new way. The mom of five was called to silence. She entered reflection and prayer. She attended daily Mass. Through cancer treatment, she was being drawn deeper and deeper into the Heart of God. She underwent harsh pruning, purification, and detachment... thereby increasing in virtue. My goodness sakes did that woman possess virtue! I've never seen such patience, such fortitude, such faith, hope, and love. Truly, she lived Holy Love in all things. Her life was God first, then others. It was unbelievable.

Then came the point where it seemed like maybe she wasn't going to beat cancer. And she had to surrender her will and accept what might be God's will, to leave this earth. Now, as a wife and mother of five, we can only imagine the battle that took place in her heart. But she did it. She surrendered. She trusted. She accepted. Before she died, she reached that place of complete peace. In the hospital, she simply said "OK," and she closed her eyes.

It was like it says in Joshua, "Once they had taken possession of it, and dwelt in it, the LORD gave them peace on every side." Friends, I believe she had taken possession of the promised land... in the center of the garden!! She had been grafted to the Tree of Life. She had found union with her God. She reached sainthood. I am sure of it. She heard the word Victory at the beginning of her journey -- not because she was going to have a physical victory over an illness. She heard the word victory because God was leading her to an eternal victory.

Before she died, she called me one night after going to adoration of the Blessed Sacrament. A bunch of us were praying a "Victory Novena," nine days of prayer, asking for the intercession of Our Lady of Victory. It was the last day of the novena, I believe. She went to the chapel with her husband, Dean. She said she was kneeling before the Blessed Sacrament, and she saw a vision. An image appeared in the monstrance, in the host. Actually, she said the host was like a hologram. She saw two images that faded back and forth, one to reveal the other.

She tried to explain to me what she saw over the phone, but then finally just said, "I will draw it and email it to you." I saved that email and that picture and would like to share them with you now.

Dear Stacy,

I attached a rough sketch of what I saw yesterday. Jesus' back was upright, and there was a pole next to him. He was not in agony and not attached to the pole and not bending over. .. I felt he was kneeling next to the pole.

I googled images of Jesus' scourging at the pillar, and there are several images of Him attached to a short pole and kneeling... I strongly feel that He was showing me that he HAD been scourged, but it was over.

When I looked at the Blessed Sacrament in a certain way, the image of Jesus kneeling would then fade, and an image of a Mountain and the Cross would be

This is the sketch that Patti drew. If you notice, she drew it on the back of the victory novena.

Friends, what she saw was this garden!! She saw the circular garden of the Lord, in a round host, in the real presence of the Lord. She saw the gate of Mary near the outer edge. She saw purification, the mountain, and the victory!

It was a prophetic image of her journey. That day in adoration, Jesus was showing her where she was and where she was headed.

So if you're asking, "what does the Victory look like?" It looks like my dear friend, Patti Kirschner, who has worked so many miracles in my life since she passed away.

If you want to experience this victory, too, I encourage you to take this to heart. Literally. Make it a regular habit to enter the garden. Begin to live there. Begin to see events and situations as part of the journey, as part of God's will. And begin to surrender to the will of God in all things.

Meditation

"Embrace My Will, child. Embrace your cross. Embrace, with love, those who I have put in your life… and simply come to Me. When you think of Me, you embrace Me. When you choose Me, you embrace Me. Resist the devil for love of Me. Resist yourself for love of Me. Resist the world for love of Me. This enables our union, little heart. Our time together solidifies it." *(An excerpt from "Mornings with my Father" by Stacy.)*

Prayer

"Lord God, enkindle me -- a little match --in the fire of Your Heart. Let me sit with you and burn for you. Consume me entirely and dissolve my will completely, that I may unite with you for all eternity. This is my earnest desire. In Your Name, Lord Jesus, I pray. Amen.

Scripture

"For I am convinced that neither death, nor life, nor angels, nor principalities, nor present things, nor future things, nor powers, nor height, nor depth, nor any other creature will be able to separate us from the love of God in Christ Jesus our Lord." (Romans 8:38-39)

Question for Reflection

Have you been praying about something (or for something) for a long time with no answer? What is it?

Ask yourself if God is waiting for a yes in your life. If it seems the clock of progress has stopped, if it seems you're standing still on the path, perhaps there is an area of your life that He wants you to surrender to Him. Maybe it's an unhealthy habit, a relationship, a sin, a way of thinking. Perhaps it's your fear. Perhaps you just don't trust Him as you should. Maybe He's just waiting for you to say, "OK, Thy Will be done."

Chapter Nine: The Call

"Draw then your final conclusion and realization of the impact of my coming to you. I come to call every soul to Holy Love and across the bridge of reconciliation. I call my children to follow me in docility traversing the abyss in faith. At the end is victory. At the end is the triumph of the United Hearts."

~ Blessed Mother to Maureen, June 18, 1997

Well, here we are, almost to the end of your DIY retreat. I hope that it's been fruitful for you thus far.   It's been an amazing experience for me, writing it. In fact, I'd like to tell you a little story about how this all came about. This topic has been something that's been brewing inside of me for a very long time.

It was 2006 when I first discovered Holy Love Ministries. I had recently started praying the rosary regularly, and I remember those days vividly. Something was taking place within me -- a stirring or a rousing. Really, it was so much more than that, but I don't know how else to describe it. There was a fire growing inside of me.

This feeling was so powerful, so overwhelming, so consuming. I couldn't escape it, and I didn't know what to do with it. So I went to see our Pastor for some counsel.

That day, Father talked to me about St. Francis of Assisi. While praying, St. Francis heard the Lord say to him, "Rebuild my church." So, he went around fixing up local church buildings that were falling apart. Later, though, Francis realized God did not mean the buildings. He meant the people. "Rebuild my Church" meant "rebuild my people."

Now, it was interesting that Father was talking to me about St. Francis. For one, my middle name is Francis. (Father did not know this.) I was named after my grandpa Frank, so my name is even spelled like the male version. Two, I chose Francis as my confirmation name. (Father did not know this either.) He did not know that St. Francis had always been very, very special to me.

Father then mentioned another Francis -- yep, you guessed it -- St. Francis de Sales, who at the time, I was not very familiar with. Come to find out, St. Francis de Sales is the patron saint of writers. Father suggested that I ask for his intercession. He even gave me a drawing of St. Francis de Sales, and....... wait for it...... he gave me a copy of St. Francis de Sales' book, *"Introduction to the Devout Life,"* that I've been referencing throughout these pages.

That book, I discovered, was very similar to the messages given to Maureen Sweeney Kyle. It was similar to the book *Interior Castle* by St. Teresa of Avila. It was similar to my prayer journal, where God was teaching me about the garden. Everything was coming together, like pieces to a puzzle, and I heard the words echo deep in my soul, "Rebuild my Church."

Over the years, this message has been building inside of me— growing strength like fierce water that continually rises behind a small dam. So I know with absolute certainty that I have been called to share this with you. But, friends, understand that you've been called too.

When you finish this retreat, you can't just close up this book and pretend like it never happened. You can't just go back to normal... especially now, during these times.

The year 2017 marked the 100th anniversary of the Fatima apparitions and the revelation of the Triumph of the Immaculate Heart of Mary. In 1917, the Blessed Mother spoke to three children living in Fatima, Portugal, about the current battle we face today: the general loss of faith, the loss of many souls, wars, and destruction. But She also promised a Triumph -- the spiritual transformation of the entire world, when all hearts will return to Her Son.

So as not to impede this Triumph, She asked for two things: the consecration of Russia to Her Immaculate Heart and Eucharistic reparation on First Saturdays. The First Saturday devotion consists of doing four things on the first Saturday of every month for at least five consecutive months:

1. going to confession
2. reciting the rosary
3. keeping the Blessed Mother company in meditation for 15 minutes
4. receiving the Eucharist

"If my desires are heeded," She told the Fatima children, "Russia will be converted, and there will be peace; if not, Russia will spread her errors through all the world, promoting persecutions against the Church. The good will be martyred, and the Holy Father will have much to suffer; various nations will be annihilated ...In the end, My Immaculate Heart will triumph."

What does this have to do with you and me, right now, 100 years later?

Friends, the Victory that I've been talking about throughout this book is the Triumph Mary was talking about in Fatima. It is the union of God and man, the transformation of every human heart into holiness. It is the transformation of the Church and the world at large. And this will all take place in the garden.

Consider this your invitation. You are being called to participate in the Triumph. You have a unique responsibility to become a temple of God's glory, which will directly impact everyone in your life. Let the sweetness of your virtue attract other souls. Let the light of God living within you inspire other hearts.

Your light is meant for this world. It has a very unique place to fill. You become a spark -- and that spark lights another, which lights another until the whole world is CONSUMED by the love of God.

In Scripture, Jesus said, *"I have come to set the earth on fire, and how I wish it were already blazing! There is a baptism with which I must be baptized, and how great is my anguish until it is accomplished!" (Luke 12:49-50)*

But it won't be easy. At first, not all will follow you to the garden or see the importance of this journey. Jesus continued in the gospel of Luke, *"Do you think that I have come to establish peace on the earth? No, I tell you, but rather division. From now on, a household of five will be divided, three against two and two against three; a father will be divided against his son and a son against his father, a mother against her daughter and a daughter against her mother, a mother-in-law against her daughter-in-law and a daughter-in-law against her mother-in-law." (Luke 12:51-53)*

Friends, not only do you have to do battle against the flesh, against the devil and his demons, but you will also likely be in opposition with some friends and family, just like Jesus warned. Not all will accept the garden. Not all will pursue this "narrow way" -- not even among Christians. Many are quite content walking the way that is wide and leads to destruction. (Matthew 7:13-14)

Many will refuse to enter the door. Many will hate the light instead of hating the grass stains. Many will not be able to prioritize love of God above all else, then neighbor as self. Many will run from the confessional and purposely dislodge gateposts.

These days, the devil is working so hard against souls, trying to dismantle the church, perverting truth, keeping hearts in bondage. Who will rise up and fight against him? Who will embrace the light within so as to scatter darkness?? In a world where sin is down-played, embraced, and made into law.... who will pursue holiness?

Sometimes I think we get so focused on everything that is going on out there in the world -- problems, divisions. It's one thing after another. And we lose our focus on the journey. We set our relationship with God aside to deal with these other things. Then, we end up out by the gate or on the outer limits. There, we shout our prayers to God over great distances, begging him, "Please, fix this. Help me."

But maybe, what we need to do is just get to the center of the garden. Maybe what we need to do is focus on uniting with Him and being in union with Him. Then, it will be as St. Paul said, "It's no longer I who live but Christ who lives in me." (Galatians 2:20)

Then, we don't need to shout over distances. In fact, we don't need to do anything at all. We just need to be. If Christ lives in me, I simply take Christ to the world that needs Him. I don't need to shout because when you're that close to Him, He hears the heart. No words are necessary.

Friends, the answer to everything we suffer -- every trial and strife -- is right here inside of us, in Jesus.

St. Teresa of Avila explained, "when [the devil] sees that the soul is completely surrendered to the [Lord]...he is afraid of such a soul...he knows by experience that if he attempts anything of the kind he will come out very much the loser and the soul will achieve a corresponding gain." (Pg. 82)

I said at the beginning of this book that the garden is important. This is another reason why. This is how things are going to change, how the devil will be defeated in the world. In the beginning, I talked about going into a "safe haven." It may have seemed like I was talking about escaping the world by going within. But we're not escaping it. We're fixing it, one heart at a time.

So, I want to encourage you when you finish this book to go to the garden. Each day, focus on *that*. Focus on Jesus, your journey, uniting with Him. Go to confession, dig up the weeds, and be fully present in every moment. Walk in Holy Love, practice virtue, and accept the will of God in all things. Begin to make this a priority, and I promise you: everything else will fall into place.

If you don't do this now... well, you will not be able to avoid the garden forever. If you don't put forth the work here on earth, then the work will be much more difficult when you die. If you die in a state of grace but are nowhere near the center yet, the

Lord will set fire to the garden at your judgment. You will still make the rest of the journey to union with Him, but it will be made in the flames of Purgatory, and it will be painful.

On Memorial Day in 2007, Maureen was visited by Alanus, her guardian angel. He led her, mystically, along a path that seemed to be covered in brambles. They went up a little incline, and he asked Maureen to stand beside him on the edge of a rocky cliff. He motioned with a sweep of his arm, and below them was a big canyon. At one end were great flames. According to Maureen, it looked like people in silhouettes bobbing up and down in flames. "There were loud cries for mercy and shouts of pain," she said, "but it did not alleviate the suffering."

Alanus told her, "These are the souls in greatest need of prayer and sacrifice. This is the lowest part of Purgatory--the part closest to Hell itself. Many suffer here, for no one prays for them. They were regarded as 'good'--some even 'holy'--in their lifetime, but it was all a facade. Many priests are among these poor souls, for they were not faithful to the precepts of the Church. There are those who lied about others and destroyed their reputations. These are them."

He showed her souls who were having molten lead poured down their throats. It burned holes through their necks but did not stop. On a ledge around the fire were many angels--more than Maureen could count.

Alanus told her, "These are the guardian angels of those poor souls being purified at this level. Through all of this suffering, the souls' greatest trial is separation from God."

Maureen saw souls who seemed to have their flesh melting away. This, too, was unending. Alanus told her, "These are the ones who were guilty of sins of the flesh."

They then moved on to view the next level. Maureen said there seemed to be something like water being poured down on the fire, so the flames were smaller--not as intense. Alanus told her, "Blood and water from the Side of Jesus continually flow upon the souls on this level."

"The souls were suffering," Maureen said, "but all their suffering seemed more alike, and for some reason, the souls seemed more united. They had their hands raised towards an opening. They seemed to be begging for mercy.

Alanus told her, "They suffer intensely for not being in God's Presence."

They moved on to what seemed like a much better area. These souls looked more like people, but they were gray. Alanus said, "These are the ones closest to Paradise. They are almost completely purified. They need maybe one Mass, or one rosary; maybe one Hail Mary to enter eternal joy."

"So you see, decorating graves is not what souls, long deceased, cry out for. Many spend long centuries in Purgatory, for their loved ones think they are in Heaven. If you pray and sacrifice for these holy souls, they will assist you now and at the hour of your death." (May 28, 2007)

So, friends, the choice is ours. We can use our free will and our faculties to choose holiness here on earth. Or, we can choose to be purified in the fires of Purgatory. But one way or the other, we must experience purification and illumination prior to union with Almighty God. It is entirely up to us, though, how and where the purification and illumination take place.

And remember, in Purgatory, it does not affect other souls. Your progress does not make an impression on other people. You will eventually arrive at Heavenly victory, yes, but you do not participate in the Triumph, to which you have been called here on earth.

So, it is important to begin now. And I know it will be hard to continue this on your own after you close this book. For this reason, I advise you to make this retreat again, perhaps annually. Perhaps during advent, in preparation for the coming of the Lord. Everyone needs a refresher.

To conclude, I would like to take one last walk through the garden with you by using the below meditation that I actually wrote while I was in the garden several years ago. I encourage you to read it slowly and really think about it. Envision it. Go there. Perhaps even make it a daily meditation.

Lastly, I want to thank you, friends, for walking with me in this book. Thank you for persevering to the end and accepting the call. May the Lord bless you abundantly in each remaining step. May you find grace, strength, and perseverance. And may we see each other again, in the end, in the victor's camp. Peace be with you all.

Prayer, Meditation, and Spiritual Communion:

Come Holy Spirit, come. Come by means of the most powerful intercession of the Blessed Virgin Mary, Thy well-beloved Spouse. My Lord and my God, I come to you, and I knock. I believe in Your presence -- which is everywhere, in everything -- in all of creation. I trust in Your Goodness, for You have promised never to leave me or forsake me, but rather, to come to me and make Your home in me.

Therefore, it is with great confidence that I knock upon the door of Your Heart and step into Your holy presence. I come, into the deep, into the secret garden within. I have journeyed along a difficult road. I have met many roadblocks, detours, valleys, and climbs. The enemy has stalked me, tormented me, followed on my heels.

Along the way, I have discovered many heartaches, many fears, many woes... each one I have picked up and tucked down into the backpack of my heart. It has made for a heavy load, Lord. But here I am now. I have arrived at a rest stop: the secret garden of our meeting. I have knocked, and You have opened unto me.

It is beautiful here -- plush, green, alive. There is stillness and light. Peace fills the air. The Blessed Virgin Mary welcomes me. She takes my heavy pack with great care and kindness. She takes me by the hand and leads me to You.

You are sitting on a rock, by a stream of Living Water, a rod and staff sit beside You. You smile and speak my name. The Blessed Virgin Mary takes my pack and begins to lay its contents at Your feet. First, there is my greatest heartache.

"I give it to you, my Lord."

Then the other heartaches, one by one. "They, too, are yours, Lord."

She then pulls out each of my fears and lays them before You. I am embarrassed there are so many. "Take them, Lord. I don't want them."

Finally, She takes out each of the woes I have encountered along the way: unfortunate situations, broken relationships, petitions, needs, and many sins. "Take these, too, my Lord."

With gentleness and love, She lays them before You. She kisses Your feet and smiles the sweetest smile. She rises and stands by my side—her arm and Her mantle wrap around me. I stand like I am under Her wing. "Do whatever He tells you," She whispers.

All that She has laid before You begins to slowly rise as if drawn to You by the magnetic force of Your Love. All that was once heavy upon me now floats before You. It is consumed. It dissipates, into Your Heart, into the fire of Your Mercy.

"Do not ask for these back," You tell me. "I will tend to them now." You point to the stream of Living Water. "Drink, child, and live," You say.

I reach down into the water and draw out a small portion into my hands, and I drink. The power of the Holy Spirit comes upon me, refreshing my soul, renewing my body. In an instant, I am made new. I am healed.

I rise to my feet. The Blessed Virgin Mary gives me my empty pack. It is as light as air. You place Your right hand upon my head and anoint me with sweet oil. You take from within Yourself, a piece of bread... a small host. You hold it up before me.

"Take. Eat. This is My Body," You say.

I fall to my knees. "Lord, I am not worthy that You should enter under my roof, but only say the word, and my soul shall be healed."

"Whoever eats of this bread will live forever," You tell me. "For I am the Bread of Life." You place the host upon my tongue. Your Light and Your Life consume me. You are with me. You are in me. I am overwhelmed with Your Love, overflowing with Your Mercy.

I rise for the journey. I do not fear the Valley of the Shadow of Death. I can do all things through Christ who strengthens me. Alleluia, alleluia.

For more information on the Holy Love messages given to Maureen Sweeney Kyle, please visit www.HolyLove.org.

www.ingramcontent.com/pod-product-compliance
Lightning Source LLC
Chambersburg PA
CBHW061319120726
48001CB00002B/593